Interpretation of Historic Sites

ABOUT THE SERIES
The American Association for State and Local History Book Series publishes technical and professional information for those who practice and support history, and addresses issues critical to the field of state and local history. To submit a proposal or manuscript to the series, please request proposal guidelines from AASLH headquarters: AASLH Book Series, 1717 Church St., Nashville, Tennessee 37203. Telephone: (615) 320-3203. Fax: (615) 327-9013. Web site: www.aaslh.org.

ABOUT THE ORGANIZATION
The American Association for State and Local History (AASLH) is a nonprofit educational organization dedicated to advancing knowledge, understanding, and appreciation of local history in the United States and Canada. In addition to sponsorship of this book series, the Association publishes the periodical *History News*, a newsletter, technical leaflets and reports, and other materials; confers prizes and awards in recognition of outstanding achievement in the field; and supports a broad education program and other activities designed to help members work more effectively. To join the organization, contact: Membership Director, AASLH, 1717 Church St., Nashville, Tennessee 37203.

Interpretation of Historic Sites

Second Edition, Revised

WILLIAM T. ALDERSON AND
SHIRLEY PAYNE LOW

A Division of
ROWMAN & LITTLEFIELD PUBLISHERS, INC.
Walnut Creek • Lanham • New York • Toronto • Oxford

ALTAMIRA PRESS
A division of Rowman & Littlefield Publishers, Inc.
1630 North Main Street, #367; Walnut Creek, CA 94596
www.altamirapress.com

Rowman & Littlefield Publishers, Inc.
A wholly owned subsidiary of
The Rowman & Littlefield Publishing Group, Inc.
4501 Forbes Boulevard, Suite 200; Lanham, MD 20706

PO Box 317; Oxford; OX2 9RU, UK

British Library Cataloguing in Publication Information Available

Library of Congress Cataloging-in-Publication Data

Alderson, William T. (William Thomas), 1926–
   Interpretation of historic sites / William T. Alderson and Shirley Payne
   Low.—2nd ed., rev.
      p. cm.—(American Association for State and Local History book series)
   Published in cooperation with the American Association for State and Local
   History. Originally published: Nashville, Tenn: American Association for
   State and Local History, 1985.
   Includes bibliographical references and index.
   ISBN 0-7619-9162-X (pbk. : alk. paper)
      1. Historic sites—Interpretive programs—United States. I. Low, Shirley Payne.
   II. American Association for State and Local History. III. Title. IV. Series.
   E159.A36   1996
   973—dc20   96-1396
                                                                            CIP
Printed in the United States of America

⊖™ The paper used in this publication meets the minimum requirements of
American National Standard for Information Sciences—Permanence of Paper for
Printed Library Materials, ANSI/NISO Z39.48–1992.

Contents

Preface

THE cause of interpretation has advanced significantly during the nine years since the first publication of this book. Though the body of literature on interpretation is still small, there are now many new books and articles that have increased our understanding of the subject. Important new work on the way people learn in historic sites and museums may soon add to our abilities as interpreters. Some sites are experimenting with new techniques of interpretation. The American Association for State and Local History continues to emphasize the interpretation of history, both in its seminar series and through its independent study unit by Norman L. Wilson and Jay Anderson on *Basic Interpretation of Historic Sites.* Perhaps most significant is the creation of a new separate classification of "historic sites" by the Accreditation Commission of the American Association of Museums. In developing the criteria for this new classification, the historic sites subcommittee identified interpretation as the single most important requirement. Clearly, the time has arrived, after nine years and four printings, to bring out a revised edition that reflects the progress that has been made.

As with the first edition, we have benefited greatly from the kindness of interpreters and site managers throughout the country, who gladly shared their knowledge and expertise with us. Although we cannot name them all, we would like to mention William J. Tramposch, Director of Interpretive Education and Special Program Officer of Colonial Williamsburg Foundation, who was particularly helpful with thoughtful suggestions on presenting the site and on the training of interpreters; Robert C. Birney, of Colonial Williamsburg, who shared with us some of his expertise in evaluation and many ideas on the subject; Bill Murray, who has dreamed big—and well—for Living History Farms in Des Moines; John W. Harbour, Jr., William B.

Pfeifer, and Renee Friedman of Sleepy Hollow Restorations; Claude E. McKinney, Dean of the School of Design at North Carolina State University; Mildred C. Compton, Director Emeritus of the Children's Museum in Indianapolis; Scott T. Swank of the Winterthur Museum and Gardens; Darrel A. Apps and Suzanne Knowles of Longwood Gardens; Rosemary Krill, formerly of the Hagley Museum; and the graduate students in Museum Studies at the University of Delaware, and especially Robert Hyland, Christopher Bensch, Nancy Bossler, Gail Dennis, Barry Kessler, Linda Pittman, Valencia Libby, and Frances Clark, all of whom did special projects in interpretation.

Others who shared ideas include Irene U. Burnham, consultant to the Valley Forge Historical Society; Brenda Milkofsky of the Connecticut River Foundation; Marion Nelson of the Norwegian-American Museum in Decorah, Iowa; Michael Ripton, Nancy Kolb, and Daniel B. Reibel of the Pennsylvania Historical and Museum Commission; John Evans Harbour of Old World Wisconsin (now Director of Mount Vernon); Jay Anderson of Utah State University; William B. Worthen, Jr., of the Arkansas Territorial Restoration; Carl and Paula Degen of Harper's Ferry; Barbara Riley of the Museum of Man in Ottawa; Donald Friary of Historic Deerfield, Inc.; Barnes Riznik of Grove Farm; Roger Fortin of Xavier University; George MacBeath of the Provincial Government of New Brunswick; James Thomas of Shakertown at Pleasant Hill; Michael Rierson of the Fairfax County Park Authority; Mary Ann Brendel, Director of Historical Interpretation Department, Colonial Williamsburg Foundation; Cynthia S. Burns and William W. Cole, Educational Specialists, Colonial Williamsburg Foundation; Mary Wiseman, Program Presentation Instructor, The Company of Colonial Performers, Colonial Williamsburg Foundation; and William Seale, scholar and consultant, of Alexandria, Virginia.

W.T.A.
S.P.L.

Preface to the First Edition

THIS book, in many respects, is only a beginning. It is an effort to begin to fill a notable, even glaring, gap in the literature of the historic preservation movement. As we approach the tenth anniversary of the Historic Preservation Act of 1966 and the golden anniversary of the beginning of Colonial Williamsburg, our only important book on interpretation is still Freeman Tilden's *Interpreting Our Heritage* (Chapel Hill: University of North Carolina Press, 1957), which treats very ably the principles of interpretation, particularly as they apply to natural history and national parks, but provides only limited help to the historic site administrator.

Our concern is not with the principles and psychology of interpretation, but with the very practical problems of developing and conducting interpretive programs at historic sites. It has not been our purpose to produce a definitive book on interpretation; a definitive treatment is impossible until more professional interpreters write and publish the results of their efforts. Neither has it been our purpose to tell the reader how to restore a historic site correctly, even though lack of authenticity in restoration is one of the most difficult problems of the interpretive effort.

From the outset, we have intended this for all historic sites, regardless of size and budget. To that end, we have traveled throughout the United States and Canada in order to see and evaluate interpretation as it is carried on by a wide variety of historical organizations. What we have tried to present in this book is the best of what we have seen. That the best has often been seen in some of the large and well-financed institutions does not alter the fact that there are many dedicated and hard-working staffs of small, less affluent institutions who are out-performing their more prestigious colleagues. In our view, it is a "cop-out" for any site to rationalize not establishing an interpretive program because "we don't have Williamsburg's budget." It can be done; we have seen it. Consequently, we have described the elements of what we consider an ideal but essentially practical program for the average site, with the expectation that many sites may not have the resources to do it all now, but with the hope that knowing what constitutes good interpretation will give them goals for future improvement.

There are a number of aspects of interpretation that we should have liked to explore, had there been adequate published materials from which to generalize. There are some interesting efforts to provide more effective interpretation for racial and ethnic minorities. There are special problems in interpreting for deaf, blind, and handicapped persons. A visit to Poland reinforced, for one of us, the need for special interpretation for people who don't speak the language. More needs to be written about interpretation as a component of craft demonstrations, sales counters, publicity, public relations, community outreach, and a number of other historical agency programs.

We should add a word about terminology. As is the case in most relatively new fields of endeavor, historic preservation does not yet have a recognized vocabulary of terms that have universally accepted meanings. Thus, what should we call what we are interpreting? Some people use the term *historic house museum,* but that does not include structures other than houses, nor can it apply to battlefields or restored villages. Moreover, the word *museum* suggests to the general public the display of objects in case exhibits. The term *historic landmarks* could not be used without risk of confusion with the special qualitative official designation used by the National Park Service in identifying structures of major national importance. *Historic restorations* might have been used, but this might have implied exclusion both of reconstructed buildings and of preserved structures and areas that are so important in our field. Faced with having to make a choice, we decided on *historic sites.* In the dictionary sense, *historic site* means the place or setting of an event, thereby fully meeting all the requirements we are seeking. It is also a term that has been in common currency among historical administrators for many years. We use it, therefore, to mean houses, other structures, and geographic areas that are notable either because of their association with a historical personage or event, or because they reflect the culture or taste of a historical period.

This book could not have been done without the generous sharing of information that is characteristic of our profession. Countless directors and interpreters at sites throughout North America welcomed us to their sites and discussed their interpretation efforts since we first began planning the book a decade ago. They are too numerous to list, but we gladly acknowledge our indebtedness to them. At least as numerous and equally helpful have been the participants at AASLH and Williamsburg seminars, whose probing questions in class and, more importantly, in bull sessions have sharpened our thinking about the interpretive process. Several colleagues have been particularly helpful. Thomas G. McCaskey, Elliot W. Jayne, William B. Pfeifer, and Elizabeth P. Callis of Colonial Williamsburg helped at several stages in the research for the book. Barbara B. Beaman of Colonial Williamsburg read and made important suggestions for improvement of the chapter on "School Tours." Mary Claire Bradshaw, former director of Gunston Hall, and Mary Tyler Cheek of Stratford Hall provided interpretive materials upon which we have drawn for the study. Carl Degen and his audiovisual staff at the Harpers Ferry Interpretation Center of the National Park Service were characteristically generous sources of information. Daniel and Patricia Reibel of Old Economy read the first draft of the manuscript and made a number of useful suggestions. James R. Short of Colonial Williamsburg worked with us in the planning stages of the project, read the completed manuscript during a summer vacation, and was an enormous help in improving the final draft. Frank Barnes, the just retired Chief of Interpretation, Mid-Atlantic Region, of the National Park Service, also read the entire manuscript, made numerous suggestions, and through some of his typically searching questions helped us to bring some elements into better focus. The shortcomings of the book are our own responsibility, of course, but there would have been more of them had it not been for the help of our fellow interpreters.

Finally, we wish to acknowledge our sincere gratitude to the Council of the American Association for State and Local History, which granted its director's request for a two-month sabbatical without which the writing and editing of the book would have been impossible, and to the Smithsonian Institution, which awarded us a National Museum Act grant in support of the travel, research, and writing that was involved. We hope the book fulfills their mission of advancing the profession.

W.T.A.
S.P.L.

Interpretation
of Historic Sites

1

Interpretation: An Introduction

INTERPRETATION is both a program and an activity. The program establishes a set of objectives for the things we want our visitors to understand; the activity has to do with the skills and techniques by which that understanding is created. The distinction between the two has not been clearly defined.

The historic sites subcommittee of the American Association of Museums defined interpretation, for purposes of accreditation, as "a planned effort to create for the visitor an understanding of the history and significance of events, people, and objects with which the site is associated." On the other hand, Freeman J. Tilden, the pioneering author of *Interpreting Our Heritage*, defined it as "an educational activity which aims to reveal meanings and relationships through the use of original objects, by firsthand experience, and by illustrative media, rather than simply to communicate factual information."

Are the two definitions contradictory? We think not. They basically say the same thing: For true understanding, more is required than the communication of factual information; understanding will occur only if meanings and relationships have been revealed. The only difference in definitions is that one describes *a planned effort* and the other an *activity*, since one is a program and the other a process by which the program is carried out.

Both are necessary to historic site interpretation. The activity of revealing meanings and relationships is essential to understanding, but without a program, the activity lacks direction. Without planning, interpreters could waste time in creating a visitor's complete understanding of secondary or minor details. Understanding the upper South's cotton culture during the early nineteenth century is useful to the visitor experience, but if that visitor leaves Andrew Jackson's Hermitage without an understanding of Jackson, the whole reason for the site's existence has been thwarted. Similarly, if we have objectives, but do not reveal the meanings and relationships that lead to understanding, we have also failed.

Most visitors require help to gain an understanding of a site. Here, interpreters introduce themselves to a visiting family. —*Mystic Seaport; photograph by Mary Anne Stets*

How well the visitor can understand the important meanings and relationships of our site depends on the program and the activity that together make up the interpretation. This includes not only the spoken, written, and audiovisual communications received from the interpretation staff, but also a variety of sensory and intellectual perceptions gleaned through the quality of restoration, authenticity of furnishings, and effectiveness of exhibits. The visitor may come to the site for a great variety of reasons, but the goal is achieved when the visitor gains an understanding of the reasons that historic site is important to the community, state, nation, world—and most of all to the individual visitor.

How much interpretation is necessary in any historic place depends in large measure upon the amount of understanding and knowledge the average visitor brings to the site. Sites that are already well known to the visitor may require little interpretation. The Battleship Arizona Memorial in Pearl Harbor requires little explanation for any person who remembers the Japanese attack on December 7, 1941, or has discussed it with someone who remembers. Yet, even for the many who may remember, interpretation can bring deeper understanding. Interpretation can help the visitor place the attack in historical perspective and may help him understand how such an attack was possible. But most Americans of the 1980s will not visit the memorial to learn these things. Their purpose in going is to satisfy their curiosity about events they remember or have heard about.

Similarly little interpretation would be necessary if a historical organization decided to preserve a typical example of an urban subdivision house. Today's visitor would understand how people live today and would not need an explanation of television sets, washing machines, air conditioners, cooking utensils, and electric lights. A restored urban dwelling of 1900, on the other hand, requires considerably more interpretation if the visitor is to leave with comparable understanding of the life styles of people of that day; and the restored house of two centuries ago requires still greater interpretive effort. The less

the visitor knows about the history of the site, the more interpretation we need to provide.

During the nineteenth-century beginnings of the historic
preservation movement in the United States, there was little
interpretation, because the average visitor had prior knowledge
of what he was seeing. Almost without exception, the first
historic sites were acquired as shrines to the great leaders of the
nation's early years, or as shrines to men who had fought in our
wars. The young nation took great pride in its accomplishments; the history of these men and events was an important
part of the school curriculum, as well as of the oral tradition.
What children did not learn from the teacher, they were told by
parents and grandparents who personally remembered the bat-
tles and leaders. Visitors to Mount Vernon did not need to be
told who George Washington was, or why he was important. He
was part of their own lives, and their visit was satisfying if they
could walk where he had walked and see the tomb in which he
was buried. Gettysburg, Shiloh, and other military parks were
then what the Pearl Harbor Memorial is to us today; if one
visitor was uninformed, the visitor by his side would be able to
tell the story.

For all but a handful of the historic sites of today, the shrine
presentation is inadequate. Times have changed. History, particularly state and local history, has been relegated to a less
important position in the curriculum. People move more often,
so that homes in which three or four generations of a family
once perpetuated the oral tradition are virtually things of the
past. The visitor to the historic site of today is both more
sophisticated and less well informed. Because he is more
widely travelled, he has had more opportunity to visit sites that
are professionally managed and interpreted; because the history
of most sites he visits is not part of his personal experience, his
oral tradition, or his formal education, he requires help if he is
to acquire understanding.

Finally, we wish to state our credo that historic sites are a part
of the national heritage and that consequently they should be
run for the benefit of the public at large. We who work for
historical agencies do not own the sites. We are trustees for

them. They are ours to restore and manage and interpret because earlier generations saved them for us; so we, in turn, have an obligation to future generations who have an equal claim to that heritage. Our trusteeship places upon us an ethical commitment to accuracy in restoration, truth in interpretation, and protection for the next generation. The financial support we receive from the public in gifts, admission fees, tax exemptions, and government payments reinforces our obligations to the people. We do not meet that obligation just by saving and restoring a historic site. Only when the essential meaning of the site and of the people and events associated with it is communicated to the visitor can we truly say that we have met our responsibilities.

2

Setting Objectives

IF historic preservation followed neat, logical patterns of action, the proposed interpretation of a historic site would be worked out, at least in outline, before the historic structure was ever acquired. In that ideal situation, the preservation group would have surveyed all of the historical structures in the area. It would have done research on the most important of those structures and would have determined which of them ought to be saved because of their potential importance in helping people understand their heritage. It would then have acquired the site knowing in advance exactly what was intended to be accomplished for the good of the community, the state, and even the nation by the enormous investment that every historic site requires.

That would be the ideal. But the realities of the preservation movement are quite different. Seldom are historic buildings saved because a group of knowledgeable people, armed with detailed research reports, has reached a dispassionate and logical conclusion that a building ought to be acquired. The usual sequence of events is that an old and revered structure of the community is suddenly threatened with destruction. Preservationists are faced with the need for immediate action. There is no opportunity to stop for several years while determining whether that particular building is the best one of its type and therefore most worthy of preservation. There is no time to decide in advance what its true historical importance may be and whether that importance, as interpreted to the public, is worth the expense of purchase, restoration, and future operation. Action must be taken immediately. And so battle lines are drawn and fund-raising begins, and with perseverance and luck, the preservation group finally receives title to the property.

With the building having been acquired, the preservation group must decide what to do with it. Very often the group decides to restore the building to its condition, appearance, and state of furnishings at some particular time in the past, and then open it to the public. The restored site thus becomes a means of communicating to visitors something about that past, and it is this use of the site that we are primarily concerned with in this handbook. But there is another potential use that should be mentioned.

This is what preservationists call adaptive use. What is usually meant by the term is that the building is used for private or commercial purposes that are essentially unrelated to the history of the building or its former occupants. The conversion of the Carmelite convent in San Juan, Puerto Rico, into the El Convento Hotel is a good example. Usually, there are restrictions on alterations or modifications of the structure that would affect its historical appearance or its potential for restoration at a later date. Occasionally, there are provisions for public visitation to the site.

But there is another kind of adaptive use, one in which the building is open to the public for aesthetic, cultural, or historical purposes other than those of a restoration. The Park-McCullough House in Bennington, Vermont, is a community cultural center that incorporates some restored historic rooms. For many years, the first building of the long defunct University of Nashville was used for a natural history museum. The Harrison Gray Otis house in Boston became the headquarters for the Society for the Preservation of New England Antiquities as well as a museum house.

In still another adaptive use, a historic building can be utilized as a museum of furniture or the decorative arts—a use that we must carefully distinguish from the historical restoration. It is easy to confuse the two, since, in both instances, the rooms of the building are furnished as if to be lived in. But while the historical restoration is an attempt to present rooms as they once actually appeared or typically might have appeared, the museum of decorative arts usually presents a connoisseur's collection of furniture that is so arranged as to please the aesthetic taste. Its period rooms are a curatorial presentation of the best that might have been, not a recreation of anything that either was or even is likely to have been. The Henry Francis du Pont Winterthur Museum is our best example of a museum of the decorative arts in a historic building.

The Park-McCullough House in Bennington, Vermont, has been adapted as a community cultural center.—*Park McCullough House Association*

If we may assume that the preservation group has considered the various adaptive uses described above and has tentatively decided to do a historical restoration, we must hope that they will be able to resist the pressures of the community to begin immediately on the restoration work. Careful planning is essential. Thorough research must be done to develop both the facts and the relationship of those facts upon which the restoration will be based and upon which the future interpretation of the house will be developed. Consultants will likely be needed to help solve problems that are new to the preservation group and to building and landscape architects, archaeologists, and other professionals who may be involved in the project.

To begin a program of restoration, we must first understand why the site was saved—or, to be more precise, why it is appropriate to be restored. The two are not necessarily the same, and the second is more important than the first. The building may have been saved for reasons that have little to do with its real historical importance. It may have been the finest old home in town. Its destruction might have left the town square without its most beautiful structure. Many people may have believed the house was designed by the famous architect who did the state capitol. It may have been saved simply because it was available at a time when a new historic site group was looking for a project.

Reasons of this sort may be quite valid for the saving of structures, but if no other importance can be found than mere age or sentiment, or even beauty (as compared to true architectural distinction), the preservation group would be well advised to consider adaptive use instead of restoration.

When considering the restoration of a building as a historic site that will be open to the public, the emotional fervor of the preservation effort must be replaced by the cool logic of historical research and the hardheaded and sometimes painful self-examination involved in making a business decision. The first steps should not be restoration and the recruiting of guides, but research and the recruiting of facts.

What, in truth, do we really know about the structure? Most historical buildings are surrounded by myths. Legend has it that the building was constructed in 1853, but is that so? Does it really stand on the site of the first log cabin built in the area? How much of the building is original? What do we know about the successive owners of the property? Was it really designed by the architect of the state capitol? It will take time to verify these statements in back files of newspapers, in diaries and letters of persons who lived or visited in the house, in deeds, wills, and other legal documents. Perhaps there are extant photographs of the building, or paintings that will show architectural details. Perhaps archaeologists can tell us something about the location of outbuildings that were once on the grounds, or of building wings that have been demolished. The number of queries is virtually endless, and the search for provable facts about the house is as full of excitement as the solving of a mystery. Usually, the truth is more enthralling than the legends that have grown up over the years.

Once we have gathered all the facts we can discover about the house, we are ready to evaluate it for its restoration potential. Two important decisions will have to be made. First, is the site really important enough to justify the expense of restoration and operation? Does its importance go beyond the town boundaries? Or need to? Is it likely to attract enough visitors to help finance operating costs out of admission fees? In short, is the story we can tell through it important enough and have we a reasonable enough assurance of long-term funding that we should proceed with plans for restoration?

Our other major decision will be determining our objectives in restoring the site and opening it to the public. Usually, there will be a number of objectives, not just one. But it is vitally important that one of these objectives by our primary goal and that the other objectives be not only secondary but entirely compatible with the primary ones. It will help to clarify planning if all historic sites are thought of as fitting into three broad categories based upon their primary purpose.

The first of these categories is the *documentary site*. By this term we mean that the primary objective of the site is to document an important historical event or the life or lives of a person or family. This usually—but not always—means that we should do our utmost to restore the structure or place to its precise condition at a specific point in time. It is not essential that every facet of the restoration be provable, but there must be a minimum of conjecture in the restoration decisions. Examples of documentary sites are numerous. Sagamore Hill, the home of Theodore Roosevelt, is an example. It has been painstakingly

The Hermitage documents the life and interests of President Andrew Jackson—*Ladies' Hermitage Association; photograph by Bill LeFevor*

restored to its condition in Roosevelt's time, and the site does an effective job of documenting for the visitor the life and character of its owner. Another example is the Raleigh Tavern in Williamsburg, which, even though a reconstruction of the original tavern, is a faithful presentation of what the Raleigh Tavern looked like when the dissolved Virginia House of Burgesses convened there in 1774 to consider resistance to Britain's Intolerable Acts.

Our second category is the *representative site.* The primary objective of the representative site is not to help the visitor understand a specific person or event, but to help him understand a period of history or a way of life. Thus, the site does not have to have been associated with a historic event or persons; what it must do is typify many other sites of its period. Its restoration should be based upon research no less careful than that for the documentary site. It may very well be restored to its precise condition at a specific time in the past. It is no less historical than the documentary site. The key difference is that the site is primarily focused on a period in the past and the people who lived in that period. Only secondarily is its focus on a specific person who may have lived in it or on a specific

An interpretation of soap making attracts visitor interest at Van Cortlandt Manor, a representative site. — *Sleepy Hollow Restorations*

historical event that may have occurred at it. The documentary site, of course, reverses these priorities.

Returning to the example of the Raleigh Tavern, it may be pointed out that its purpose is to show the visitor a specific tavern as it existed at a time when the meetings that were held in it gave the tavern particular importance in the history of the American Revolution. Its primary purpose is not to portray a typical tavern of the period, but to show a specific tavern that was once so historic that its reconstruction was essential to Colonial Williamsburg. The interpretation of the Raleigh focuses on the historical events that took place in it, not on its typicality, notwithstanding the fact that a tour of the Raleigh will, in fact, help the visitor understand something about the place of the tavern in colonial life. By contrast, the wonderful Bump Tavern at the Farmers Museum at Coopertown, a historic structure moved and authentically restored at its present location, is primarily representative. The objective of its interpretation is to present a nineteenth-century New York tavern as a functioning place, one that provided lodging, food, drink, and entertainment during the period.

Old Sturbridge Village is another fine example of the representative site. All of its buildings are authentic historical structures that were moved to the village from all over New England. The village itself never existed; it was created, to enable its visitors to understand something about New England town life in the first half of the nineteenth century. During a visit, we may learn the names of some of the families who originally owned its houses or ran its shops, but only incidentally. Old Sturbridge Village is presented as typical. It represents the essence of many other New England villages of its period.

Our third category is the *aesthetic site*. The classification includes structures that are appropriate for preservation because of their distinctive design and form, and historical buildings for which the interpretive focus is on aesthetic beauty rather than on history, as in the case of the documentary and representative sites. Though subtle, the distinction is important because of the interpretive objective: to present what is beautiful, not what happened in the past. Frank Lloyd Wright's "Falling Waters," may be an important document in the history of architecture, but is primarily meant to be enjoyed for its beauty. The same may be said for Cheekwood, the mansion now housing the Tennessee Fine Arts Center in Nashville.

Less clear is the example of the Winterthur Museum, which demonstrates the difficulty of such classification. When the first edition of this book was published, the Delaware mansion of Henry Francis du Pont, with two hundred rooms of furniture of the American Colonial and Early National periods, was considered to be an art museum by then-director Charles van Ravenswaay. We accordingly classified it as an aesthetic site. Its next director, James Morton Smith, took a different view and the interpretive focus shifted: the period rooms and furniture were not viewed only as works of art, but also as historical objects which could help the visitor understand the society in which they were created and used. With period rooms assembled on the basis of connoisseurship, rather than to document the past or to present what was typical, the du Pont mansion remains an aesthetic site—but one that may, in time, complete a metamorphosis and be reclassified.

When we categorize historic sites as documentary, representative, and aesthetic, we are speaking about the order of priorities for their restoration and interpretation, not about a rigidly exclusive purpose for the site. As has been shown, a documentary site may contain features that the interpreter can use in discussing how the site is representative of a whole class of structures or places, or how its owners were representative of a social or economic order. Conversely, a representative site frequently will shed some light on a historical person or event. And a documentary or representative site may well contribute to the enhancement of the visitor's aesthetic appreciation. It is vitally important, however, that those who restore and interpret the site be consistent in their priorities.

Each historic site should have a clearly defined primary objective, and all decisions made during the restoration of the site or in the development of its interpretation must be in accord with that objective. If other objectives become possible as secondary goals of the site, they may be exploited. But it is important not to

The Henry Francis du Pont home, Winterthur, features period rooms of early American furniture.—*The Henry Francis du Pont Winterthur Museum*

permit those secondary objectives to dominate in the decision making. They are legitimate only as fringe benefits.

Among specific examples, Andrew Jackson's home the Hermitage, is a documentary site. Clearly, it is a structure that should be restored to the condition in which Andrew Jackson knew it. It follows that it should show only his own taste, not a connoisseur's choice of furnishings. If he lived in a cluttered house—by today's standards—the restored site should also be cluttered. The objective of the restoration should be to help the visitor understand this particular man, husband, planter, politician, military leader, lawyer, statesman, and president. The purpose is not to portray the typical planter of his day, though we may learn much about agriculture from a visit. Neither is it a primary objective to tell us about the legal profession of Jackson's time, though we may learn something of that, too. Nor is it to show, in his house, what we, today, might consider to be the finest furniture produced in the 1830s in the Upper South, although it is our good fortune that Jackson did acquire some excellent pieces that may be pointed out to the discerning visitor. Every step of the restoration and interpretation must

At representative Pilgrim Village, visitors and interpreters haul a cart through dirt roads.—*Plimoth Plantation*

relate back to the basic objective of helping the visitor to understand Jackson as a person and as one of America's great leaders.

On the other hand, if the objective of a site is to portray typical or representative aspects of a period, it is important that the development of the site should not focus too closely on the personality and tastes of an individual. Consider how much less effective Old Sturbridge Village would be if, instead of sticking to the primary objective of collecting and assembling buildings typical of a New England town, the decision had been to place around the village green the homes of notable New Englanders. At the end of the green might have been the Old South Meeting House from Boston, and, facing it, the homes of Whittier, Longfellow, Ethan Allen, and John Adams, plus the House of Seven Gables, the barn from Brook Farm, and Thoreau's cabin from Walden Pond. How different the interpretation would now be! Instead of the visitor's learning what life was like in the typical New England town, he would be given in succession interpretations of leading literary, political, and military figures of nineteenth-century New England. And he would probably depart with all kinds of misconceptions about the intellectual level of the New England town, how Longfellow and Ethan Allen had lived side by side, and how these greats of New England history had worshipped together at the Meeting House.

Finally, the strongest warning must be reserved for giving equal value to the aesthetic objective with either the documentary or representative. This is the greatest temptation of all, because it flows so naturally from the nostalgia we feel for the past, and from our wish to honor the memory of historical figures and events. Even as we chuckle over the story of the log-cabin restoration in which tongue-and-groove oak flooring was installed out of respect for an occupant who later became a great statesman, we are more likely to be guilty of less obvious improvements almost equally distorting to the more pretentious documentary and representative sites entrusted to our care. In the face of historical evidence to the contrary, restorers of many sites have substituted their own tastes, or those of a major donor, for those of the historical past. Homes whose original owners never dreamed of any kind of foundation plantings are today adorned with English boxwood; crystal chandeliers hang where brass gas jets once were installed; white paint now covers dark-stained woodwork that would seem gloomy to modern eyes; and the furniture of yesterday's people of good taste is replaced by the selections of today's connoisseur of antiques.

This temptation to permit aesthetic considerations to overrule decisions that are right for a documentary or representative site is understandable, but its end result is to fictionalize the past. It is natural for us to want ourselves and those whom we admire to appear to best advantage. Just as we will instruct the portrait photographer to improve our image by retouching to eliminate a second chin or bags under our eyes, so we want to do everything possible to present the homes of our historical heroes to the best advantage. Instead of respecting their own taste in homes and furnishings, however, we somehow assume that, because their tastes were different from those of our own day, we have some obligation to protect them from public ridicule that surely would result if we showed the house the way it really was. In our mistaken attempt to venerate the memory of historical figures, therefore, the typical becomes atypical. Important knowledge of the past is denied the visitor; we have denied him the opportunity to reach a valid conclusion of his own.

Setting the primary objective of the restoration is the most important single decision to be made in the preservation effort. Only after setting that primary objective should we turn to the matter of establishing our secondary objectives. What other things would we like to have the public learn at our site? Have we an especially good opportunity to help the visitor understand the importance of irrigation in the West? Or subsistence farming in the South? Or mercantile trade in the Northeast? A good set of secondary objectives can increase substantially the contributions a site can make to the visitor's understanding of our heritage.

Finally, whatever objectives have been selected, they should be adopted by formal action of the board of trustees, whose responsibility it is to determine the policies that the restoration

Visitors chat with interpreters during demonstrations at Old Sturbridge Village, which represents a typical New England town of the early nineteenth century.—*Old Sturbridge Village; photograph by Robert S. Arnold*

will pursue. The objectives should then be promulgated in writing, so that every committee chairman and every association member will know precisely what direction the preservation effort will take. All members of the organization should be working toward the same goals. Once a written statement of objectives is in hand, work can proceed on the restoration. In the meantime, those who have been given the responsibility for developing the interpretation of the finished site may begin the months of planning that should precede the official opening.

3

Planning the Interpretation

IT is obviously impossible to tell every visitor to a historic site all that is known about it. Time is limited, and so is the visitor's interest. The historic site organization must therefore make a number of decisions about what information it wants to give the visitor in the time available. These decisions necessarily will stem from the objectives that have been agreed upon for the site, and they will usually result in a limited list of facts, ideas, and historical concepts that will constitute the core of the interpretation.

The wisdom of this approach to interpretive planning is obvious. The site was saved and restored because it had historical value; it is therefore important that the visitor understand what that value was. He must also understand what the historical value *is* today—and the site organization should recognize at the outset that historical value is not something fixed for all time, but something changing with new perspectives and new audiences. The visitor may depart with other information and perceptions, but for him to depart without understanding the historical value is to negate the entire purpose of the preservation effort.

The determination of informational and conceptual objectives for the interpretation flows directly out of the statement of objectives for the site, and is usually developed by the staff and approved by the board of directors. The staff will then decide generally what historical subjects will be included in the interpretation—nineteenth-century agricultural history, daily life on the mining frontier, decorative arts of the Mennonites—and what historical concepts should be taught—the doctrine of self-government, the rise of the common man, the urbanization of the nation. The staff will then determine where, when, and how these subjects and concepts will be worked into the interpretation.

Administrative control over the general form and content of the interpretation is very important. Without it, there will likely be a wide variation in the information given out by various members of the interpretive staff. One group of visitors will learn about furniture, the next about agriculture, and the next about politics. A more serious consequence will be the development of legends and serious errors of fact, as new guides learn from older guides without the benefit of carefully developed guidelines.

There are some administrators, to be sure, who believe that each interpreter should develop his own interpretations. They maintain that administrative guidelines stifle spontaneity and are likely to result in an offensive "canned spiel" interpretation. It may be argued, however, that the truly gifted interpreter will be effective with or without guidelines, and that the untalented interpreter will soon turn to his own or someone else's canned spiel, regardless of the opportunities for spontaneity.

In the great majority of cases, the advantages are clearly on the side of developing a standard interpretation aimed at the site's audience and centered around predetermined objectives concerning what facts the visitors should learn and what ideas and concepts they should understand as a result of their visit to the site. Interpreters should receive guidance on where to present these facts and concepts most effectively. Every interpreter should follow the major points of emphasis in the interpretation, but in his own individual way, using different anecdotes to illustrate basic points, varying choices of words, and adapting the basic material to the obvious interests of the group.

Who the Visitors Are

Until fairly recently, most historic site visitors were people who brought to the site some understanding of the historic events that took place there. Visitors at today's sites no longer come with as much—or, sometimes, with any—historical

Why visitors visit is an important question for historic site administrators. Above, molasses making is one attraction for the crowd
attending the annual Tennessee Fall Homecoming.—*Museum of
Appalachia*

knowledge. They come not to pay homage, but to satisfy nos-
talgic feelings about the past, to enjoy themselves, to learn,
and—for a few—because visiting sites is "the thing to do." And
they present the historic sites with new challenges, foremost
among them being the need to interpret.

What are these visitors like? Unfortunately, we have little
precise information about them; the number of historic sites
that conduct marketing surveys of their visitors is much too
small. A recent survey by the Colonial Williamsburg Foundation provides figures that may apply to other sites—or, in some
instances, may prove unique.

Of family, pleasure, or vacation visitors, people under age 25
account for only 6.1 percent of the total; those between 25 and
55 are more evenly distributed, though younger ages are
favored; and about 20 percent are 55 or older. The number of

men and women are about equal. In the area of education, 10 percent have a high school diploma or less; 11 percent have a doctoral degree, and an amazing 75 percent have a college degree or some post-graduate education. Some 21 percent report having visited other historic sites. Overall, 17 percent report incomes exceeding $50,000 while 20 percent earn less than $20,000. More than half (51 percent) visited the site for the first time, and 71 percent intend to return.

For tour visitors (bus, air, train), the statistics are somewhat different. There is an even distribution within the age brackets of 25 to 55, and a substantial 42.3 percent are older than 55. Nearly 47 percent report college degrees or some post-graduate education, while 27 percent have a high school diploma or less. None earn incomes of more than $50,000, and 43 percent report incomes of $20,000 or less. Female visitors account for 69 percent of the total.

Among all visitors, 25 percent come to Williamsburg upon the recommendation of a friend—a testimonial to word-of-mouth advertising and an inducement to provide good interpretation. It is also interesting to note that women are significantly more active in planning the visit than are men.

Many of today's historic site visitors have been to other sites. They are accustomed to professional interpretation. They will encourage their friends to visit a historic site only if their own visit has been satisfactory. Historic site organizations of today must consider carefully the sophistication of their visitors. Organizational and civic pride are at stake, as well as future visitation.

In considering who the visitors are, one should also be aware that different seasons of the year may bring different types of people. For example, more children visit sites with family groups in April, July, and August than at other times of the year, because during those months most schools either have spring vacation or are not in session. Another Colonial Williamsburg survey concludes that parents traveling with their children learned far more of what Colonial Williamsburg hoped they would learn than did those who traveled without children. Since children tend to ask more questions, it may be that their parents learn from the answers. It may also be that parents study in advance of the trip to be able to answer the children's questions themselves.

Finally, we should note that the average educational level of all visitors has increased in recent years—along with that of the general public—and that the educational level for tourists in the school vacation periods is higher than it is during the rest of the year. Perhaps this is fortunate for the interpreter; during the peak tourist seasons, when the sites are most crowded and hurried, visitors may be correspondingly quicker to understand what they are seeing and hearing.

Why the Visitors Come

One of our biggest handicaps in interpretation is lack of knowledge about why people visit historic sites. Very few sites have attempted audience surveys, and those that have done so have obtained results that are of only limited help to other sites. What we know about the motivations of our visitors is largely subjective. It is based for the most part upon impressions received by historic site administrators during their casual observations of tourists. Clearly, nostalgia is one of the prime motivations. Many people have a romantic view of a past that they believe was less hurried and more relaxed than the time in which they now live. They minimize or ignore the hardships of the past—hardships that, by the way, are seldom interpreted at the sites. Instead, visitors contrast the best of the past with some of the worst of our own jet-paced, plastic, and computerized age. For many visitors, then, the historic site is a form of escape.

Other visitors appear to be searching for their cultural roots and for a sense of belonging. They want to experience the sense of continuity that the site can help provide as a tangible link with the past. Many parents who bring their children to historic sites seem to have a sense of this continuity, already; their visit is an effort to help create that same sense in their children.

It would be unrealistic to assume that all visitors have a serious purpose. For many, the historic site is another form of

Visitors are most concerned with how people from an earlier age lived. Here, an interpreter cards wool as she describes the homelife of the nineteenth century.—*State Historical Society of Wisconsin*

entertainment, something different to do on a long weekend, a place to see old furnishings and furniture. The historic site visit, however, has the special appeal of being an entertainment that personally involves the visitor—especially if the interpreter helps the visitor relate to what is said. Visitor involvement in the interpretation of historic sites is in marked contrast to the silent, spectator role they have so often experienced.

One final observation should be made about the motivations of the visitors. Regardless of the frivolousness or seriousness of their purpose, what seems to interest visitors most is people. They are inordinately curious about how people of an earlier era lived, what they ate and wore, what they worked at, what they did for entertainment; how, in short, the lives of the people who were associated with the site compare with the life styles of today.

Developing Interpretation of Historic Sites

What kind of interpretation should be developed? Remembering that the goal of interpretation is understanding, good interpretation will help visitors understand what the site can reveal about the importance of people and events connected with it, about a way of life, or about the cultural tastes of the past. It consists of what is shown, said, or done that will help those visitors experience a personal involvement and a sense of identification with their heritage. It includes not only the person-to-person relationship between visitor and interpreter, but also the visitors' learning experiences through museum exhibits, audiovisual devices, labels, interpretive markers, living history programs, craft demonstrations, and publications. It is not, as some sites' administrations seem to forget, the story of how an Aunt Martha of one of the board members donated the sideboard, how much it cost to restore the falling ceiling, or a series of object identifications: "This is an apple-peeler. This is a Chippendale chair. This is a foot-warmer."

For interpretation to meet professional standards, it must conform to a set of generally accepted principles.

Research. First of all, interpretation must be based on research. Someone with research training or experience should go through all pertinent manuscripts, records, newspapers, and books to get facts about the site and should then evaluate these facts and draw acceptable conclusions from them. The reports on that research should be available to every person who has any responsibility for the interpretation of the site. A trained historian—either paid or volunteer—should oversee this research work if at all possible, but much of the work can be done by volunteers. Their help could prove to be invaluable.

Knowledge of the site may require archaeological research. If so, the work should be done by a trained archaeologist who knows how to make excavations, catalogue the artifacts that are discovered, make comparisons with the documentary evidence, and produce the final reports for the interpreter's use. Highly skilled amateurs can do this work, sometimes; but be careful— an unskilled amateur can irretrievably destroy the very evidence you are after.

People with curatorial training or experience should examine both the documentary and the archaeological evidence to determine how the building was probably furnished. They should also be advisors in the search for the site's original furnishings, if they are available, for authentic period pieces that research indicates might have been used, or for good reproductions of pieces that were characteristic of the period. The evidence for the furnishings, as well as a list of furnishings, should be made available to interpreters.

Architects with special training in architectural history, preferably with experience in restoration work, should analyze the structure itself, noting probable dates for the original construction and changes that have been made over the years. They should then plan the work that will be necessary to restore the structure to its original appearance. Again, their reports should be made available to the interpreters.

It is not always feasible for small organizations to pay for the extensive research that is needed for authentic presentation of the site to the public. But there are alternatives. There is no good reason why several small sites in the same general area cannot pool their resources and employ skilled outside consultants who can instruct and guide volunteer members in some of the research work and who can then help evaluate the findings. Sometimes there are graduate students or professors from nearby universities who will undertake part-time work. There may also be retired professionals in the area who would be willing to share their skills and talents in research in order to help historic sites achieve authenticity. Finally, don't overlook the possibility that dedicated amateurs may be willing to inform themselves sufficiently to make valuable contributions to some part of the needed research.

When the many facts have been gathered, there is one remaining step yet to be taken, that of analysis. Without it, the facts are a jumble of items that enable us to get only part of the way to truth. The rest of the way is the task of a historian who is trained to relate the facts to one another, to place events in a larger perspective than just the community in which the site is located, to relate local events to natural-social-political environmental factors, and to other historic sites in the area. With sound analysis of the facts, we shall hope to arrive at what the court oaths refer to as "the truth, the whole truth, and nothing but the truth."

Organization. Many of us can recall high school or college courses that stressed the value of making outlines for speeches and compositions. There were major points that had to be of equal value and were expressed in parallel form, and there were subpoints that supported or elaborated upon the major points and also had to be of equal value and expressed in parallel form. These basic principles apply as well to the interpretation of historic sites. We must think through the main points we want to cover, in order to accomplish the objectives the administration has set for the historic site. To accomplish this, there should be, at the beginning of every tour of a historic site, a general introduction covering the main points of importance. These main points, in turn, should be developed in appropriate places as the tour progresses and as each area, its use, furnishings, architecture, and other elements may suggest. The major points should be summarized briefly at the end of the tour, so that visitors are reminded of the importance of the site.

Accuracy. The visiting public has the right to expect that what they are seeing and hearing at a historic site is the truth. That does not mean that the interpretation has to be dull. Usually, there is an abundance of true details that can enliven an interpretation without sacrificing the truth. It may take time for interpreters to dig them out of the research reports, but it will be time well spent.

Good interpretation does not glamorize the historic site nor indulge in hero worship at the expense of truth. It tells the story as it was, without indulging in fantasy or creating events that never happened. Throughout the Upper South and Border states, for example, there are many sites at which visitors are shown or told about the entrance to a now-collapsed tunnel once used to escape from Indian attacks or to move slaves on the Underground Railroad, when the truth is that they are looking at a root cellar. Finally, good interpreters should not give ecstatic reviews about how "beautiful" or "wonderful" everything is; they should present the information and leave the ecstasy to the guests.

Good taste. Interpretation should be in good taste. The historic building itself and what is said about it should be a quality production. Both should avoid being cheap, sensational, or vulgar. Interpreters, for example, should resist the temptation to attract attention or entertain visitors by telling off-color stories or by using language that might offend or embarrass guests. Neither should they play up sensational features of the site at the expense of more important aspects of the interpretation. Trying to impress visitors with how much some particular antique has cost is also in bad taste, and is an open invitation to any would-be thief. Interpreters should never try to impress their audience with their own knowledge, nor should they provoke laughter by ridiculing the past. A good interpreter does not have to resort to "jazzing up" his presentation to make the site attractive to visitors.

Secondary objectives. Good interpretation must be based upon decisions the historic site organization has made, both about its primary objective and about the secondary objectives it has decided are consistent with the major purpose. These secondary objectives are usually a combination of historical facts and historical concepts, from which it is hoped visitors will learn and understand. The development of these secondary objectives is extremely important; and, once decided upon, they must be put into writing, so that they will be available to each person who has interpretive responsibility for the site.

Facts and Concepts about a Historic Person

It may be helpful to study some examples of these statements of objectives. If we were developing an interpretation of a documentary site once owned by an important historical person, we might want the public to learn the following *facts* about that person:

Person's background
    Family, the area in which he or she grew up, influences, education
Profession or trade
    Preparation for it, accomplishments, his or her influence
Tastes
    In architecture, furnishings, gardens, hobbies, etc.
Importance of the individual
    Accomplishments, thinking, influence

Visitors should also have an understanding of basic *concepts* that are important in the life of the individual:

This area was a land of opportunity.
He or she was dedicated to certain basic rights of humanity.
He or she was a real person, as real as you or I.
He or she made a difference in the history of this country.

Facts and Concepts about a Historic Event

In developing an interpretation of a documentary site involving a historic event, we would want visitors to learn the following *facts* about the event:

Different points of view,
What led up to this event
What really happened
Who was involved
What was going on elsewhere at the time
What difference the event made in history
The relation of the event to other occurrences in the area

Again, we would hope that visitors would leave the site with an understanding of the following *concepts:*

The importance of the event
The relevance of the event to the present
The value of preserving such a site

Facts and Concepts about a Representative Site

In setting objectives for the interpretation of a representative site, we would want visitors to learn such *facts* as the following:

Characteristics of the society represented
Family life, education, social life, religion, sports, amusements, how people made a living.

Appearances of the homes and public buildings
Use of furnishings, tools, equipment
Comparison of the way of life at this site with that depicted at other sites in the area

Then we would hope that visitors would leave the site with an understanding of such *concepts* as:
Basic needs of people in every age are similar; each age takes care of those needs in its own way. This site represents a way characteristic of its period.

The way we think about certain issues today is influenced by the way these people thought about issues similar to our own.

Facts and Concepts about an Aesthetic Site

In developing an interpretation of an aesthetic site, we would want visitors to learn *facts* about:

> Furniture styles, ceramics, fabrics, metals, etc.
> Architectural details
> Landscape architectural details

And we would hope they might understand such *concepts* as the following:

> Styles are a reflection of culture and affluence of the society that creates them.
> The craftsmanship and artistry of this particular period differ from that of the postindustrial era in important ways.

If one person is going to conduct a group all the way through a site, that person can be permitted a good deal of flexibility as to exactly where certain points should be covered, provided all major points are eventually developed in some logical fashion. On the other hand, if the group receives its interpretation from a succession of interpreters in different areas—or stations, as they are usually called—it becomes essential that specific points be covered in designated areas. If this is not done, major points will be left out entirely, or visitors will be subjected to undue repetition.

In establishing objectives for a historic site, the administration should determine what emphasis is to be made and suggest both a proper organization for the interpretation and indicate the best areas at which to develop major points. If this is not done, the results can be disastrous. To illustrate this, Mary Claire Bradshaw, former Manager-Curator of Gunston Hall, concocted the following example of what might happen.

A TOUR OF GUNSTON HALL: THE HARD WAY

Hallway

Hi. Would you like a tour—or would you rather just look around?

Where are you all from? South Dakota? I have a cousin in South Dakota.

Well, I can tell you about some of these things. George Mason was a very important man in the eighteenth century. He had a lot of money.

This clock is a grandfather's clock. The portrait here is one of his sons. He is supposed to have gone mad in his old age and died having a fit in the garden.

Study

This was the sitting room. That's George Mason's sister, over the mantel. This table is on loan from the Virginia Historical Society. That's a Rhode Island secretary, given by the Colonial Dames of Rhode Island. That's a foot-warmer, by the fireplace, and over the door are antlers from a deer George Mason is supposed to have shot with one bullet.

Dining Room

That's George Mason's portrait—or, rather, a copy of it. Those are Chippendale chairs by the table—I've got a set like that.

They used to have curtains in here, but they took them down. Now, I don't know why they took them down.

If there is anything you want to know about, just ask me.

Parlor

That's Mrs. Mason, over the mantel. She died very young. We won't be able to all get in here at once. Mr. Mason married again. This room is one of the one hundred most beautiful in America.

About the bowl? I don't really know. I'm only here on Tuesdays.

You can see a tea table. They drank a lot of tea.

Master Bedroom

This is the master bedroom. They put all their kids upstairs—I guess for privacy. Somebody told me the other day George Mason had wooden false teeth—just like George Washington.

It should be noted that this is only a partial tour of Gunston Hall, but it illustrates what can happen without proper guidance. Consider how painfully familiar this presentation is.

Living History Interpretation

There has been much discussion in recent years about "living history." The term has been applied both to a method of interpretation and—less successfully—to a new category of museums. Most historic site interpretation is done through verbal interchange between interpreter and visitor. The living history approach, however, seeks to impart understanding to the visitor by having interpreters assume and re-enact the roles of people who might have participated in events associated with the site. At its purest, as found at the Conner Prairie Museum or Plimoth Plantation, the visitor enters a world in which there is no history beyond the date of the site: interpreters consistently disclaim knowledge of events that lie beyond that date.

At the other end of the scale, it is less clear when we can say with assurance that a "living history" interpretation is taking place. Is the site that intersperses traditional interpretation with craft demonstrations doing a living history interpretation? Does a craft demonstration by a person in modern dress constitute

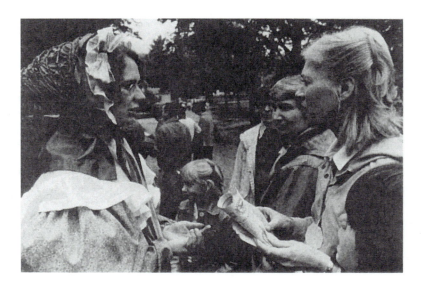

Whether or not interpreters will wear costumes is a planning decision faced by site administrators. Here, a costumed interpreter answers visitors' questions.—*Old Sturbridge Village; photograph by Robert S. Arnold*

Costumes should be as correct as possible.—*Atlanta Historical Society, Inc.*

living history? Are costumed hostesses who make no attempt at role-playing nonetheless engaged in living history interpretation? And *how much living history does there have to be* to classify our site as a living history museum, rather than just a historic site?

Leaving aside the problems of definition, it suffices for our purposes to recognize that living history is a field of growing interest, and that it works best for representative sites that attempt to interpret a way of life. For the documentary site, dealing with specific events and people, the living history elements of costuming and role-playing have advantages and pitfalls that need to be addressed.

Costuming

One of the important planning decisions is whether to put the interpreters in costume. Many historic sites find that there is a heightened sense of realism if interpretation is done by people attired in period dress. Costumed guides are an important part of the overall visual image at Old Sturbridge Village, the Farmer's Museum, Plimoth Plantation, and other sites. They look as if they belong in the historical setting, and they help to make the setting look right for its period.

The costume also sets the interpreter apart from the visitors, visually. This is important in several ways. It makes the visitor comfortable to have a recognizable person in charge. It also helps the interpreter enforce rules and security measures, because the costume clearly denotes a member of the staff.

Costuming has its problems, however, and many site administrators oppose it on practical grounds. They prefer to have interpreters in uniforms or in streetwear that has sufficient uniformity to establish the authority of the wearer. Costuming, they argue, is expensive. Moreover, a lot of the costuming one sees at historic sites is more quaint than correct. One soon-to-be-open commercial site, for example, announced that its guides would be authentically costumed; and the press release then explained that elements of each guide's costume would be authentic reproductions of apparel

In their roles as innkeeper and blacksmith's wife, interpreters weave baskets in Prairietown, an 1836 historic village.—*Conner Prairie Pioneer Settlement*

worn in the seventeenth, eighteenth, and nineteenth centuries! Finally, opponents of costuming believe that visitors feel freer to ask questions of a guide who is dressed the same way they are—an argument, incidentally, that pro-costume administrators vigorously dispute.

Whether a site has costumed guides is a matter of personal taste and financial ability. But if the decision is in favor of costuming, those costumes should be as correct as possible, not only for the period and the activity being performed, but also in all their details. Satin dinner dresses should not be worn by the kitchen interpreter, nor cotton bonnets in the drawing room, nor sneakers with either. And not only should the costume elements be correct, but, ideally, so should hair styles, makeup, watches, accessories, and even eyeglasses. The public has a right to expect authenticity if there is costuming of the interpreters. If costuming cannot be done correctly it probably ought to be avoided and the money used for other elements of the interpretation.

Role-Playing: The Interpreter

Costumes are essential, of course, if the site expects its interpreters not only to tell their story, but also to act the part of people who lived in the historical period of the site. Whether there should be such role-playing, either planned or unplanned, is a matter of considerable discussion in the profession. Guides wearing their own clothes or a modern uniform usually tell a straight story of the site without losing themselves in a role of the period. Interpreters in costume, on the other hand, may unconsciously do a bit of role-playing, even though they are primarily telling a straight story about the past. There is something about a costume, particularly if it is authentic, that gives the wearer a sense of being a part of another era. William E. Marshall, former director of the State Historical Society of Colorado, reports that authentically costumed interpreters at the restored Healy House very quickly adopted physical mannerisms of the period, such as walking, sitting, and climbing stairs in the fashion of the nineteenth century. They also began to use nineteenth-century colloquialisms and speech habits. So influential is the costume that the interpreters soon were speaking as if they and the house were back in that earlier period. "They cooked this way" thus becomes, in the interpretation, "We cook this way." This kind of role-playing, done under careful supervision, can enhance the visitors' experience.

Some historic sites enrich their interpretation by planned role-playing. In this situation, the interpreter, working in authentic costume of the period, should use the accent and language characteristic of the person portrayed, speaking always in the first person. Needless to say, it takes a talented actor to perform role-playing of this type. One example of such role-playing is given by a National Park Service interpreter at the Appomattox Court House National Historic Site. He portrays a young man making his way back to a farm in the Valley of Virginia following General Lee's surrender at Appomattox. Dressed in tattered homespun, he carries the gun that he has used in the war, leans against a Civil War cannon, and speaks with the dialect of a young farmer with little education and with limited knowledge of all that was involved in the recent struggle between the North and the South. In speaking about his experiences and in answering questions asked by visitors, he is very careful to speak only in the first person and to make statements that only a man of his background and rank would know. He gives this performance several times each day during the summer as a supplement to the regular interpretations.

Role-playing can add a great deal of reality to a historic site and can help involve visitors in the past. But it must be very skillfully performed, or it will be banal. Moreover, role-playing can tell only part of the story of a historic site; the role-player, after all, can only know one or two aspects of the story, and those only from the standpoint of a contemporary of the events being interpreted. There is still a need for the regular types of interpretation told in the third person by well-trained and skillful interpreters. Role-playing should be thought of as a supplemental device to be used when there are people available who have the talent to create effective dialogue and to perform with the skills necessary to make the roles believable.

In the book bindery at Colonial Williamsburg, guests participate in the process of marbling paper for book linings.—*Colonial Williamsburg Foundation*

Role-Playing: The Visitor

Role-playing need not be confined to the interpretive staff. Many sites provide opportunities for their visitors to assume roles, as well. In these cases, the visitor himself is given a momentary or partial opportunity to play a role of another period in time. This can be done with either the visitor or the interpreter participating, and sometimes with both. For example, a visitor can have a sense of reliving the past by being allowed to do something that would have been done during the period represented. Some historic sites—the Farmer's Museum at Cooperstown, for instance—allow visitors to try their hands at churning butter or using woodworking tools. Some visitors do a sort of role-playing by riding in old wagons or carriages, being towed down a canal in a barge, riding an old-time train pulled by a snorting steam engine, or by being allowed to shoot

An anxious visitor waits to taste a pie flavored with garden herbs.—
Shaker Village, Shakertown at Pleasant Hill

an ancient muzzle-loader. Other visitors try to relive a bit of the
past by wearing part of a costume—a coonskin hat or an actual
dress from the period represented. It is interesting, too, to observe that visitors enjoy role-playing vicariously. Even if only

one of the group is allowed to use some antique device, the whole group somehow feels involved. The past becomes more real for them.

A word of caution should be given about role-playing by visitors. While they might enjoy totally voluntary role-playing, they can easily be intimidated if they feel pressure to do so, particularly in front of an audience. The theoretical benefits of involvement can disintegrate in the clutches of embarrassment, or in the resentment over being treated as a "character," when they really wanted to look and listen.

Administrators of historic sites should also remember that, helpful as living history programs are in depicting the atmosphere of the past, they cannot communicate a full understanding of what the site represents. Living history programs are best used as supplementary to the usual conducted tours. A truly good interpreter can bring a historic site alive without wearing a costume or role-playing.

Summary

Developing general outlines for the interpretation of the historic site is a major responsibility of top-level staff members, working within the general objectives that have been agreed upon by the trustees. It is not a task to be delegated to the interpreters themselves, though it would be a short-sighted administrator who did not enlist the interpreters to help in the task.

The planning must begin with research. It is difficult enough to interpret what we know; it is impossible to interpret what we do not know. Once the facts are assembled and analyzed, our next step must be to determine who our audience is. Only then can planning decisions be made about the priority facts and concepts that are to be communicated, where in the site they should be interpreted, and whether costuming and role-playing should be part of the interpretive approach. Successful interpretation begins with setting clear objectives and requires careful planning to achieve those objectives. But ultimately, of course, it depends upon the skills and the abilities of the interpreters themselves.

4

Presenting the Site

THE culmination of all the discussions of objectives and all the planning of the interpretation is the presentation of the site to the visitor. All the investment of money and time in the acquisition and restoration of the site, all the efforts in research and planning are at stake as the visitors enter the site. If they are made welcome and are given a tour that has real substance, they will depart having learned what the site represents, and they will be word-of-mouth advertisers for growing visitation through the coming years. If, on the other hand, they receive brusque treatment and a perfunctory tour of little or no substance, the site will be a failure. The key to success is the visit itself, and this means, in most cases, the effectiveness of the interpreter.

Opening the Building

An organization that is administering a historic site has an obligation to open it on a regular basis on specific days at designated hours. Preferably, a house should be open daily on a year-round basis, even though there may be periods in the winter months when visitation is so light that such a schedule may seem scarcely worthwhile. During summer months, some consideration should be given to extending the hours of opening if there is heavy visitation. This accommodates more visitors and enables some of them to enjoy the site in the cool of the evening. Daily opening should be assumed if there are directional and advertising signs on the highways. Unless these signs indicate otherwise, the traveling public that has been lured off the main-traveled routes has a right to expect to visit the site at the end of their detour. But this is not always the case; some very small historic sites operate on such an informal basis that whether they are open at all depends upon the whims of their volunteers. Others close the site to visitors in order to hold parties or membership meetings. This is grossly unfair to visitors who may have no other opportunity to visit the site, and they are certainly not going to recommend such a place to their friends.

Well-planned directional signs are important, both for inviting visitation and for helping visitors find what they want to see. Signs should be of a consistent design that creates a quality image for the site, and located wherever pedestrians or drivers might become uncertain about reaching their destination. Keep the message brief, and the letters large enough for easy reading. Use arrows or other clear directions (*next left*, *exit here*, *entrance only*). Try to avoid statements that require expensive seasonal—or even annual—changes.

It is important that the staff actually open the historic site at the specified hour. Few things are more annoying for a visitor—particularly a visitor on a tight schedule—than to arrive at a historic site at the hour advertised for opening, only to find the doors closed. Too often, after waiting for what may seem an incredible long time, the visitor finally sees guides arriving breathless and quite unready to begin the day's work. Then follows a demonstration of historic-site mechanics, as guides bustle about shutting off burglar alarms, counting tickets and cash, and arguing over who is to do what. Meanwhile, enthusiasm for the visit may have disappeared because of the wasted travel time.

This again points up the need for working out procedures for handling groups ahead of time so that the guides know what they are to do and so the visitor will not be neglected.

Gathering groups. The whole tone of the tour can be set when visitors are being gathered into a group. If the guide is gracious and helpful, visitors are likely to relax and have an enjoyable tour; if the guide is curt and impatient, visitors are likely to have an unhappy experience throughout the tour.

Visitors do not like to stand in line for long periods of time waiting to enter the site, nor do they like to be ignored. On extremely busy days, both irritants may be difficult to avoid, but a good interpreter can make the delay seem shorter. First, visitors should always be told how long they are going to have to wait for their tour; and why. Then, if possible, the interpreter or another staff person should stay with them, chatting informally about such things as where they are from, whether this is their first visit, and what other places they have visited. The interpreter should also use this opportunity to tell guests about things of interest that can be seen from that particular spot, or something connected with the historic site that ordinarily would not be discussed during a regular tour. He should also give visitors a chance to ask questions.

Many historic sites give visitors printed brochures to read while they are waiting for the tour to begin. This not only occupies their time, but also helps prepare them for a greater understanding of the tour. Old Sturbridge Village has gone a step further by passing out a questionnaire which guests seem to enjoy answering.

If the gathering area for visitors is not treated as a restored room of the site, consideration may be given to the creation of exhibits that visitors may look at while they are waiting. A photographic exhibit of the site before, during, and after restoration is frequently of great interest. Other exhibits may display archaeological objects, documents relating to the site, photographs of its earlier occupants, paintings and prints, or family possessions not easily shown in the restored portions of the site. A slide show or audio recordings either of voice or period music can also help, as can a planned tour of the grounds (in good weather!).

Some large historic sites make use of "life on the scene" to entertain guests standing in line: a town crier calling out the "latest advices"; a strolling minstrel singing songs appropriate to the period of the site; a juggler showing his skill; children rolling hoops and playing skittles; an oxcart slowly plodding by; craftsmen demonstrating a craft. There are any number of appropriate activities that can hold the visitors' attention while they are waiting to enter an exhibition and help them forget the necessary waiting period.

An interpreter uses a simple ploy to hold the attention of waiting visitors.—*Colonial Williamsburg Foundation*

A small historic site with few visitors would do well to consider holding those newly arrived briefly in the area where the conducted tour begins for possible later arrivals. The first visitors should not be kept waiting for more than five minutes but should move on through the site, regardless of how small the group is.

This practice has a number of advantages. The interpreter will not be so physically tired after fewer tours through the site. He is not so likely to fall into a recitation by rote, which often results from constant repetition of the story of the historic site to a continual flow of small groups. And usually a larger group of visitors inspires a more interesting interpretation.

Some small sites have the opposite problem: too many visitors at one time during the busy season. If all of them were allowed to go into the site at the same time, obviously few of them would see very much. Equally obvious is the fact that some visitors are going to have to wait longer than the recom-

A crafts demonstration helps educate and entertain guests having to stand in line.—*Atlanta Historical Society, Inc.*

mended five minutes. Under these circumstances, a good interpreter will make a point of seeing that the group understands exactly why they have to wait and how long the wait is likely to be. And an interpreter truly concerned about the happiness of the visitors will be available to talk to them about things of special interest while they are waiting and to answer questions for which there might not be time on the tour. For example, if a good-sized group were waiting to enter a small historic church, an interpreter might well use the time to point out architectural details of the building, identify plantings nearby, mention the date of construction, name parishioners buried in the churchyard, tell how the church was named, and bring out other details which will not be covered within the church itself.

As a group gathers, interpreters should call attention to rules and restrictions for visitors. If possible, this should be done at the first station, where the introduction to the historic site is given. Guests will resent being confronted immediately with a long recital of things they cannot do, so it is better to work the rules gradually and casually into the interpretation. For example, if the first station happens to be one where visitors can be seated, a guide can make a point for future reference by saying something like this: "I am glad that you are comfortably seated. I regret to say that this is the only room in which this will be possible. Enjoy it while you can!" Or: "The artifacts that you will see throughout the site are an irreplaceable part of our heritage, and for that reason we ask that you not sit on the chairs or handle the objects."

Interpreters must enforce these rules firmly and as graciously as possible, and exercise judgment. Guests will, inevitably, infringe upon the rules and touch things they shouldn't. In most cases, a quiet reminder of the irreplaceable nature of the object should suffice. At other times, however, there may be a need for the drastic measures of a guard in Windsor Castle who, spying a youth trying to touch a priceless Royal possession, bellowed from the other end of the room: "Touch it again and I'll cut off yer 'and," which solved the problem quite nicely.

Interpreters themselves should obey the same rules imposed upon visitors. It is disconcerting for a visitor, after having been told that he must not touch anything, to see an interpreter pick up a rapidly deteriorating fan which belonged to the wife of a former president of the United States and flip it back and forth to show how it works. Only rarely should a guide handle any part of a collection. In a way, it is a reinforcement of the rules for a guide to be able to say: "I am not allowed to handle this fabric, either. We'll just have to look and imagine how it feels. The curators assure me it is as rough as it looks." or: "I've been tempted many times to pick up that cup and saucer to look at the mark on it, but it's forbidden. I guess it wouldn't stand much handling, fragile as it is."

The size of tour groups is determined by the volume of visitation at particular seasons of the year, the weather, and the intervals between tours, as well as by fire regulations, weight limits of the floors, and the need to control group conduct. In extremely busy times, groups may have to be increased in size, but they should never be so large that they cannot be kept under control or that visitors cannot see the exhibits. In addition, with small groups, there is less danger of pushing and shoving which might lead to accidents either to visitors or to the collection.

Some historic sites limit the number of visitors per day or tour by admitting only those with advance reservations. The Hearst San Simeon State Historical Monument in California, for example, requires reservations in advance except for tourists who are willing to wait for a cancellation. For three different tours of the estate, the total number of visitors is limited by available space on buses, which transport people up La Cuesta Encantada, the Enchanted Hill, to see William Randolph Hearst's magnificent home. It may be necessary to disappoint some travelers. But keeping the number of visitors down to manageable size helps to insure that those who do visit the site will have a rewarding experience.

At most historic sites, visitation increases during the summer, when families traditionally take their vacations. Some sites handle the greater number of visitors by allowing them to move through the site at their own pace, usually along a specific route. If this is allowed, interpreters or security guards should be stationed at intervals to answer questions and protect the collections. Visitors who like to "stand and stare" enjoy the freedom of the stationed tour. At some historic sites in this country, however, visitors are simply lined up and shoved through, with admonitions to "Move along, please; don't stop the line." This "herding" of the public is a great disadvantage to those who bring very little knowledge to the site and need to be given a full interpretation.

Some historic sites limit the size of groups on a year-round basis. Generally, only six people at a time are taken through the charming colonial houses of Historic Deerfield in Massachusetts. Reservations at the Winterthur Museum and Gardens must be made months ahead to see the major period rooms, and groups are limited to four people. Other rooms, shown to some-

Some sites handle greater numbers of visitors by providing alternatives to the personally conducted tour, such as allowing the guests to wander at will.—*Iowa Living History Farms, photograph by Miriam Dunlap*

what larger groups, are available to the casual visitor who arrives without reservations. Limiting the size and number of groups in this manner is a luxury that few historic sites can afford, but it is essential to the kind of interpretation Winterthur and Deerfield provide.

No matter what the size of the groups, certain tour procedures should be followed. As already stated, visitors ordinarily should not be made to wait more than five minutes for a tour to begin, even if it means that a guide will take only one or two people. Small groups should be given as full a tour as larger groups. With small groups, the interpretation can be less formal, more conversational—an approach that establishes especially good rapport.

Some historic sites have developed a compromise between the fully conducted tour and the wander-at-will type with no interpretation. This is called "stationing." Usually, the size of the groups is doubled. A short introductory interpretation is given at the first station, with directions about the exhibits— where to go next, the pattern of traffic, and the like. The first interpreter also indicates that there will be other interpreters in specified areas along the way who will discuss the history of the site and answer questions. Some historic sites have the person who starts the interpretation lead the group to the second station and give a brief interpretation and directions there, as well. When this routine is followed, as each new group goes into the exhibition, guides stationed throughout move ahead one station until they have made their way through all stations in the building. At that time, they take a break and start over again at the first station.

When stationing is used, it is important to make specific interpretations at each designated stop on the tour. Otherwise, there may be repetition or important information may be left out. The following is an example of procedures that might be developed for stationing at a site in times of heavy visitation.

PROCEDURES DURING STATIONING

There are certain times of the year when heavy visitation makes it impossible to conduct individual groups through Stratford Hall. Stationing will be used instead. This means that an interpreter will be stationed in each of the strategic rooms throughout the mansion, and as new groups arrive, each interpreter will move to the next station when the interpreter following him appears. After he has covered the final station, the interpreter will take a rest break before it is again his turn to introduce visitors to the mansion in the Law Office and to conduct them forward through the West Entrance on the second floor. Stations will be assigned by lot.

Guides will be assigned to the following stations:

   I. Law Office: three
  II. West Hallway, upstairs: one
 III. The Great Hall: one
  IV. East Hallway, upstairs: one
   V. East Outside Stairway: one
  VI. East Hallway, downstairs: one
 VII. Central Passage: one
VIII. West Hallway, downstairs: one

After a general introduction to the mansion, the first interpreter will lead the group up the west stairway into the West Hallway upstairs and talk to them about the library closet, the library, and the parlor. The person already stationed in the upstairs West Hallway will move on into the Great Hall. Each interpreter will move one station ahead following the stations listed above.

The first interpreter will instruct the group on such points as where the group goes next; the desirability of having families remain together; regulations about handling artifacts or touching walls; and the fact that other interpreters at specified stations will be available to answer questions.

After giving an interpretation in the upstairs West Hallway, the first guide will send the group on, letting them move at their own pace. When the second guide appears, the first guide will move on into the Great Hall, and so on through the stations. No guide should leave a station until another guide appears as a replacement.

Keeping groups together. At some historic sites, it is not necessary to keep visitors together as they view the exhibits. One can wander throughout Old Sturbridge Village as one pleases, for example, except for the General Salem Towne House, where visitors are taken through in groups. At New Salem, Illinois, a reconstruction of the pioneer village where

The large number of visitors at Mount Vernon necessitates stationing.—*The Mount Vernon Ladies' Association*

Lincoln lived from 1831 to 1837, visitors learn about the buildings and their uses from signs. Guides are stationed in only a few places and give very little interpretation, though they do answer questions. Many National Park sites use tape recordings and signs effectively for interpretation inside a historic site, leaving visitors free to move about as they please. At the Ford Mansion in Morristown, New Jersey, Washington's headquarters, a ranger is available to answer specific questions, but no guided tours are available except to organized school groups with reservations. The visitor has a self-guided tour, aided by excellent signs that tell the history of the house, the use of the rooms, and something about the furnishings. Visitors can follow any order they choose and linger over exhibitions which especially interest them—an example of a self-conducted tour.

And for outside historic areas, the National Park Service uses, in addition to signs, wayside exhibits about the surrounding terrain and its history, such as a "period" view of the scene and possibly a map, particularly helpful in a battlefield area.

But when there are conducted tours, and exhibits are not protected by barriers of some sort, there must be specific procedures for keeping groups together. A guide whose interpretation is genuinely interesting will usually have no difficulty holding the group's attention. Whatever instructions are necessary should be given pleasantly but with authority. Simple directions will usually work; "If you will gather around me, I'll tell you what you are going to see. Then you'll have plenty of time to look around and ask questions." Frequently, an unusual object in a room or an amusing anecdote will catch the group's attention and hold their interest.

People who wander away should be told as tactfully as possible to stay with the group. One might say, "I'm sorry, but I will have to ask you to stay with the group. This is the only way this exhibition may be shown." Unless the entire exhibition is under glass or behind impenetrable bars, there is a real threat to security if guests are allowed to wander at will without supervision. Interpreters who find that visitors stray very often may well look to the type of interpretation they are giving to be sure that it is not too long, too uninspiring or plain uninteresting.

Where interpreters stand has much to do with controlling groups. It also has a lot to do with the comfort of the group and their ability to see and hear. An interpreter may stand in a position that makes it easy for him to remain ahead of a group as he leads them from one station to another. It is wise always to be ahead of a group unless it is necessary to let them pass by so that traffic may be better controlled. This also means that the interpreter needs to create a sense of anticipation about the next room to be seen, so the group will want to keep up with him, rather than lag behind. An interpreter should stand in a position that enables him to keep the entire group under surveillance for security purposes; and he should stand so that he, not the group, faces the light. Guests should be as comfortable as possible while they listen to an interpretation. Above all, interpreters should *stand* while talking to visitors except when role-playing. It is discourteous to talk to visitors from a sitting position if they must remain standing.

Moving groups from one area to another. Groups can be moved from one area to another at the desired speed by using a statement which suggests that they are ready to proceed—such as, "When you have finished looking, we shall move on to the parlor." Or one can call attention to something of special interest ahead: the portrait of a famous person, an interesting mantel, the fireplace, a gaming board, a flower arrangement—items of interest at most historic sites are innumerable. Under no circumstances should visitors be given the impression that they are being hurried through an exhibition or cheated out of seeing all that there is to see. A relaxed manner on the part of the guide can do much to give visitors a sense of a leisurely tour, even though, during periods of heavy visitation, groups are moved at a faster than normal pace.

To keep things running smoothly, each interpreter should be conscious of the need to move his group as soon as another group approaches. Even if he has not said all that he had planned, he can complete the interpretation at another point. He can avoid making visitors feel rushed by not making such comments as "We'll have to rush along. Another group is coming!"

Doing the Interpretation

When there are only a few visitors and no on seems to be in a hurry, one can afford the luxury of a leisurely, detailed interpretation. But during very busy seasons, when the site is running over with tourists, interpretation must be shortened if all visitors are to have tours within a reasonable time following their arrival. This does not mean that the interpretation has to be skimped; but it does stress the importance of a good outline and comprehensive knowledge on the part of the interpreter. Some facts will have to be eliminated; others can be stated in fewer words. For example, in describing a historic event, the interpreter might seek a single summary word to express a long struggle: "*Reluctantly,* they decided to leave for the West" might be substituted for a detailed list of arguments pro and con that one could relate if time permitted. One can also leave out anecdotes not really necessary to the main thread of the interpretation. And many details can be reserved for answers to questions. Although an interpretation may sometimes have to be shortened, it should still emphasize the same basic points as a longer approach.

Involving visitors in the interpretation. Visitors to historic sites enjoy an interpretation much more if they are somehow involved in it. This can be done in a number of ways. One is by subtly drawing out the knowledge that visitors bring with them. While a group is gathering, an interpreter can ask where they are from, whether they have visited this site before, or how they happened to choose this area to visit. Visitors respond to this special attention. More important, the interpreter will learn something about their backgrounds and their specific knowledge of what the historic site represents, which will help him coordinate what he says to the visitors' interests. For example, "You people from Arizona will know that this area was once a part of Mexico," or "You visitors from California may be surprised to learn that one eighteenth-century Virginian wrote a friend in England saying that Virginia stretched from the Atlantic to the Pacific and included the island of California.

Visitors can also be involved through the interpreter's coordinating facts that they already know with those relevant to the site. Watch the visitors nod in assent to such expressions as "You will recall that John Adams defended the soldiers accused in the so-called 'Boston massacre'"; or "I am sure that a frying pan such as this may remind many of you of your grandmother's kitchen." On the other hand, visitors become understandably unresponsive if the interpreter tries to give the impression that he knows all there is to know.

Another way to involve visitors in the interpretation is to cultivate their sense of being on the precise spot where historic events occurred or where some well-known person lived. Visitors respond to such expressions as "You are sitting where Buffalo Bill and Wild Bill Hickock once sat . . ." "Just about here, where we are standing, the Minutemen stood and fired that 'shot heard 'round the world.'"

Visitors respond to questions, even rhetorical ones. If an interpreter says something like "Have any of you ever been to Salt Lake City?"—heads will begin to nod. "Then you will recall that Joseph Smith, the Mormon founder and leader, was murdered here at Nauvoo. You will remember that he believed. . . ." Or "Have you any idea what this might have been used for? It's a shoo-fly chair." Such rhetorical questions should not embarrass visitors if the interpreter gives the answer almost immediately. It is best to avoid difficult, direct questions which might embarrass a visitor if he doesn't know the answer.

Administrators at most historic sites have found that these interpretive techniques do not have to be varied much on a seasonal basis, excepting those months of the year when more than the usual number of family groups with children visit. Then, very definitely, interpreters should make a point of bringing into the interpretation things of special interest to children. An experienced interpreter, for example, will ask all children, excepting infants, to stay close to him, so that they can hear about an interesting object ahead (a corn-husk doll, a miniature tea set, a blunderbuss, a doll's cradle, and the like). Then, while the adults are gathering, the interpreter will talk to the children only. This is an extremely effective way to hold youngsters' interest and avoid discipline problems. Another device is to ask a child to carry an old-fashioned key or to help demonstrate how something was done in pioneer times. Asking children questions to which they are very likely to know the answers is another attention-getter—and parents listen, too. One rarely fails to get a response with "Who can tell me who the first President of the United States was?" And a good follow-up is "See whether you have a dollar bill in your pocket and then look at that portrait. Are they the same man? Who is it?"

Answering questions. Interpreters soon learn that visitors also like to ask questions; and they tend to ask the same questions, over and over. No matter how many times a day an interpreter has been asked the same questions, he should patiently give an accurate, courteous answer, each time. A good interpreter will learn to anticipate the most frequently asked questions and can incorporate the answers into his regular interpretation. If proper research has been done at a site, the answers to most of the questions will be known. These answers should be available to interpreters. It is helpful to keep in a convenient place a file box containing the most frequently asked questions, with their answers.

Interpreters often encounter embarrassed visitors, hesitant to ask questions, who feel that they should already know the answers. This is evident when the visitor begins with such a preface as "I know this is a stupid question, but. . . ." An interpreter should respond by reassuring the visitor, "Well, actually that isn't a stupid question. Many people ask that," or "No, in fact, that's a very good question. I believe all of you will be interested in the answer."

Sometimes visitors ask questions that have not been anticipated or for which research has failed to turn up an answer. When that happens, be sure to distinguish between "I don't know" and "We don't know." If an interpreter does not know the answer he should not guess at a probable one; he should simply say honestly that he doesn't (or we don't) know the answer. As a matter of fact, some visitors are delighted to find out that they are not the only ones who don't know all the answers. They also find it stimulating to learn that research is still going on, that the historic site is still trying to find answers to unanswered questions. They may even be tempted to return to the site to check the progress made in solving the mysteries.

Whenever possible, the interpreter should attempt to find the answer to the visitor's question. If an answer is not readily obtainable, an interpreter should write down the question and the visitor's name and address, and give them to the person in charge of research, who in turn should mail the answer, if it is available, to the visitor. If no answer can be obtained, the visitor should be told. Visitors respond to this courtesy and will be more likely to remember favorably the historic site that affords it.

Interpreters should answer a question with "I don't know"

only once. The next time the question is asked, they should know the answer, if an answer is obtainable.

Before leaving the matter of questions, mention should be made of the problem visitor who seeks to monopolize the interpreter's time with special-interest queries. If an interpreter senses that the answer to such questions might be of interest to the entire group, he may respond something like this: "This gentleman has asked an interesting question. All of you may be interested in hearing the answer." This enriches the interpretation for all; and by answering to the group, the interpreter prevents the special-interest visitor from taking over the tour. If the interpreter feels that no one else would be interested in the answer, he should offer to talk with the person asking numerous questions after the regular tour is completed. Then, if it develops that the visitor's questions stem from serious scholarly interests, arrangements may be made for a special tour during off hours or a slack period.

Interpreting "why" as well as "what." Even though interpretation of a historic site is based on careful research, is in good taste, is centered around predetermined objectives, and is well-organized, it still will not be meaningful to visitors unless it gives them a feeling of reality and unless they can relate to it. For example, in the interpretation of a documentary historic site, a visitor should learn not only what events occurred in this place at a specific time in history, but *why* they occurred in just this particular place and nowhere else. An interpretation based on a list of dates and a stark recital of incidents will not bring the event alive for visitors. They need to sense the issues and crises that led to these particular events, the choices available, the decisions that had to be made, the struggle between differing points of view, the personalities involved, the mounting tensions, what actually happened, and the difference those particular events made in this country or region, or even the world.

Suppose that a visitor to Old State Capitol in Springfield, Illinois, were told simply that, on June 16, 1858, Abraham Lincoln delivered his "House Divided" speech in the Hall of Representatives. That is the cold fact, but it fails to involve the visitor in the long, bitter struggle going on in the country at that time over the issues of slavery and the right to secession from the Union. It does not reveal the rivalry between the able orator, Stephen Douglas, and Abraham Lincoln for political power. It does not pave the way for the eventual choice of Lincoln as the first Republican to be elected president of the United States. It does not reveal that the statement, "A house divided against itself cannot stand, I believe this Government cannot endure permanently half slave and half free," was to echo through four bloody years of civil war and was to anticipate the issuing of one of the most important historic documents ever produced in this country, the Emancipation Proclamation, which changed the pattern of life in the United States for all time by freeing the slaves.

Only by knowing the *whys*, the *whats*, and the *results* will visitors to a historic site understand the importance of historic events and relate to them.

Presenting Different Kinds of Sites

Homes of historic persons. There are historic figures so well known in this country that it would seem unnecessary to provide very much interpretation for the houses with which they are associated. Yet even in a historic house whose owner is well known to many people, there is a need for the kind of interpretation that will bring the historic person out of the pages of the history books and reveal him as a human being.

For example, the architecture and furnishings at Monticello are carefully documented and can tell us much about Thomas Jefferson. The ingenious clock in the entrance hall, the bed conveniently installed between two rooms, the contrivance for producing more than one copy of a document at a time, and many other clever devices reveal Jefferson's inventive genius. The fine architectural details and the exquisite original furnishings tell us that this was the home of a man with cultivated tastes. But that man will not really come alive unless we can help the visitor see him in that setting, using those things.

Documented anecdotes about Jefferson's interests and habits

Thomas Jefferson's home, Monticello, reflects the tastes and interests of the nation's third president.—*Thomas Jefferson Memorial Foundation, Inc.; photograph by James Tkatch*

can put him on the scene. Such expressions as "Mr. Jefferson was accustomed . . . ," "Visitors to Monticello report that Mr. Jefferson often . . . ," and the like, help visitors to see the man himself in his home in a much more effective way than the usual "This chair belonged to Jefferson."

Nor will Jefferson emerge as the great influence he was—and still is—if only his furniture and architecture are talked about. His library, for example, might well be used to reveal him as one of the great scholars this country has produced. It also might speak of his dream of a free public school system for the children of Virginia and of his founding of the University of Virginia. Anecdotes about his relationship with such men as George Wythe and John Adams, or about the philosophers who influenced his thinking, should be told, to reveal the man who led the movement to separate church and state and who incorporated into the Declaration of Independence basic concepts of government which motivate us even today.

The possibilities of bringing such national heroes as Thomas Jefferson to life and giving them meaning and relevance to people of today are limitless if we will only free ourselves from the stereotyped "This is a Chippendale chair, this is a goffering iron, this is a foot warmer" sort of interpretation that has been all too prevalent in historic sites.

There is a somewhat different challenge in interpreting historic houses that belonged to little-known persons. If the homes of these people are interpreted solely as a collection of furnishings with proper attribution to their donors, visitors are not going to understand the kind of persons the owners were, or what went into their development, what their influence was on others, and what difference they made in their nation, region, state, and local community. Visitors may go away wondering why anyone bothered to spend the time and money to save this particular site and to open it to the public as a museum.

How many people outside of Tennessee, for example, have ever heard of John Overton? And yet, his home, Travellers' Rest, is open for visitors. It could be shown as an interesting example of the style of house constructed in Nashville in the late eighteenth century and added to, over the years, with fine furnishings such as a lawyer of the period, who lived well, would have owned. A lot of people would go away happy if Travellers' Rest were shown as this and nothing more. But they would have missed a great deal.

With proper interpretation, on the other hand, they might gain some understanding of what life in the early settlements of Tennessee was like. They might be aware of the many problems a young Overton faced, coming into the area, for example, in dealing with the Indians. Visitors might sense John Overton's influence on his friend of long standing, Andrew Jackson. They might visualize the young Overton persuading his friend Jackson to have a second wedding ceremony to legitimatize his marital relationship with Rachel Robards, who mistakenly assumed that she had been properly divorced from her first husband before marrying Jackson. Visitors well might imagine the two friends meeting here in the parlor, sometimes called the "Room of History," planning the strategy of Jackson's campaigns for the presidency. They might visualize Overton and his niece with her children who came to live with him while her husband was off fighting in the War of 1812, here in the "sitting room," the family room of the period, eating their meals, sewing, spinning cloth, cooking, and perhaps even sleeping in this one room.

A historic site associated with a person not too well known outside the immediate area will have little appeal to visitors unless, somehow, the life he lived is recreated for them and his influence made clear for them to appreciate.

The representative site. A representative site may be a collection of buildings whose intended use is to show a way of life typical of a given place at a particular time in the past, or it may be a single building presented not for its association with a historic event or personage but to show how a type or a class of people lived during an era.

If such a site is authentically furnished, its static appearance alone will say a lot about how people lived during that time that it represents in that particular place. Much more can be done to bring such a place alive by creating life on the scene. A demonstration of cooking over an open fireplace, for example, heightens the visitor's sense of reality and helps him to relate to the past. Sheep wandering about a village green, with their sounds and odors, take visitors back in time. A craftsman demonstrating a particular craft, and explaining it as he does so, conveys much more than can words alone.

Live demonstrations are not always possible; but a skilled interpreter can approximate the reality of a demonstration by telling how objects were used and for what purposes. An interpreter can describe the way a housewife of another era would have prepared a meal, for example, by showing objects she would have used and explaining their purposes. Just pointing to an object and calling it by name ("This is an apple peeler") will not stimulate the imagination nearly as much as employing

it to promote thought—what do apple peelers tell us about family consumption of apples in another era, what was the importance of apples in the diet (fresh fruit before canning and freezing), and how were fruits and vegetables stored to preserve them (root cellars).

Interpretation gains much from the use of such expressions as "It was the custom of the time for women to press the ruffles on their dresses with the use of a goffering iron such as this"; "This family Bible reminds us that religion was very much the center of these people's lives. They believed . . ."; "The tastes of the people of this period ran to ornate architecture, such as you seeing the elaborately carved moldings in this room"; "Families tended to be large during this period. The youngest children might well have slept in a trundle bed such as this. It was pulled out at night, but could be stored out of the way under the large bed during the daytime."

The aesthetic site. People who visit aesthetic sites usually have a more academic interest in furniture styles, ceramics, architectural details, and the like, than they do in historic events or personages or a way of life. Usually, they are either experts who already know a great deal about antiques and who are there to enjoy the collection and to add to their knowledge, or they are nonexperts who know very little about antiques, but are eager to learn. The experts need little direction and may be annoyed by an interpretation that attempts to "people" a room. They want time to examine details, make comparisons, and draw their own conclusions. The wise interpreter will say as little as possible to them about the exhibit, but will be available to answer questions and to respond with interest to observations the experts may make.

A group of interested beginners, on the other hand, will need interpretation that will help them to recognize styles, learn something of the influences that determined styles, and appreciate skilled craftsmanship. Again, a skilled interpreter will not

---

OPPOSITE PAGE: Demonstrations can heighten the visitor's sense of reality and sense of personal relationship with the past. Here, an interpreter demonstrates food preparation, or *foodways.—Conner Prairie Pioneer Settlement*

be particularly concerned with trying to bring an exhibit alive by showing people in action using these things; he will, instead, make use of such details as carving, shape, materials, and the like, in interpreting the pieces.

Interpreting for Foreign Visitors

In recent years, more and more people from other countries have visited historic sites in the United States. These groups present special challenges to the interpreter. The most obvious is the language barrier, but perhaps of equal importance is the challenge of interpreting our history to people with a different cultural background.

The language barrier is a difficult one. At its worst, the visitor understands little or no English, though many visitors have some familiarity with our language and require only that we take special care to talk slowly and to enunciate carefully. If an interpreter is needed, however, the site should make reasonable efforts to provide one. The responsibility to do so depends largely on the number of foreign visitors the site can normally expect: A coastal city site has a greater responsibility than an inland city, and sites near the borders of Mexico and Quebec have a special need. It is reasonable to expect some advance notice that an individual or group is coming that will require an interpreter. The foreign visitor who arrives without notice, like the tour bus that does the same, must be prepared to settle for what is possible.

If the site does not have an interpreter on staff, alternative sources will need to be explored. Sometimes a local college or high school has faculty members who can be called upon to volunteer their services. Many cities have ethnic cultural organizations whose members will help interpret, and individual citizens can sometimes be persuaded to add their names to a roster of people who can respond in an emergency. Sites that confront the language problem with any frequency might also prepare translations of introductory brochures to help orient the foreign visitor.

Cultural barriers are also difficult. Some interpreters feel apologetic, presenting a site only a century or two old to visitors whose culture goes back thousands of years; others communicate a smug pride in what our country has accomplished, overlooking our great indebtedness to the cultures from which the American people came. The skilled interpreter should be neither apologetic nor smug. It is as legitimate for foreigners to want to understand our "newness" as it is for us to want to understand their country's antiquity. The good interpreter who knows something about our cultural inheritance not only helps add to the understanding of our own citizens, but provides a communication link with the foreign visitor, to make the site more meaningful.

When accustomed to interpreting for Americans, it is easy for the interpreter to assume certain basic understandings on the part of the visitor; one doesn't have to explain concepts and events that are part of the popular culture. This is not the case with foreigners, however, for whom we may need to explain Watergate, Grand Ole Opry, the Civil War, and Cabbage Patch Dolls. Interpreters should remember this in handling foreign groups, and allow extra time so that language and cultural barriers can be overcome and understanding made possible.

Do's and Don't's of Interpretation

Interpretation of historic sites is often ruined if interpreters ignore certain basic rules, such as these.

1. Make your talk short and to the point. If you must err, do it by saying too little rather than too much.

2. Change your interpretation a bit each time you speak to visitors. If you memorize what you are going to say, like the salesman at the door who has to start all over again if he is interrupted, you may be painfully embarrassed if you "forget your lines."

3. If you make a mistake, say so and laugh it off. Visitors identify with the human qualities of an interpreter who is not infallible. Besides, the heavens won't fall.

4. Speak confidently, but never with an attitude of superi-

ority. If you are nervous speaking before the group, remember that you probably know more about the subject than they do. After all, you have access to information that they don't have.

5. Don't preach: leave that to the pulpit. Say what you have to say as well as you can and hope for the best.

6. Keep some information for questions, rather than immediately telling all you know. Visitors like to ask questions and are often likely to come up with good ones.

7. Speak in a natural, informal way, never in singsong. Try to give the impression that you just happened to think of a particular point that visitors might enjoy hearing about it.

8. Leave yourself and your personal opinions on controversial subjects out of your interpretation. Visitors did not come to hear about you, but about the site.

9. If visitors appear bored or indifferent, do evaluate what you are saying and how you are saying it. Cut it short and bring in a few of the most interesting points you've reserved for such occasions.

10. Remember that you are the historic site, so far as visitors are concerned—the front line. You can make or break visitors' interest in the site and in what it has to say to the modern world.

11. When interpreting for a foreign group, speak slowly and distinctly, resisting the impulse to speak louder than usual.

12. Give foreign groups extra time to ask the questions that will help overcome language and cultural barriers.

13. Try to link the culture of your site to that of foreign visitors, if possible.

5

Additional Methods of Interpretation

ATTENTION is usually concentrated on the human interpretation of historic sites, because, of all the means of interpretation, it is the most widely used and probably the most effective. There is no equal to the elucidation given by a trained, well-informed interpreter in a person-to-person relationship to the visitor. Nevertheless, there are other methods of interpretation that supplement or substitute for the human interpreter. For the site that, for whatever reasons, cannot provide human interpretation, other possibilities include publications, museum case exhibits, and a variety of mechanical and electronic devices. The site that already has an established guide program can supplement it effectively with these other methods of communication.

Publications

Few historic sites are without some published informational materials to distribute as visitors' aids. These publications may range from the simplest kind of giveaway leaflet to full-length books. They will vary in purpose and in content, in design, in quantity printed at any one time, and in expense of manufacture.

Brochures and leaflets. Simplest of the publications is the brochure or leaflet. A single-sheet publication with one or more folds, the leaflet usually serves three different purposes. It is used to promote visitation to the site, usually through tourist bureaus, motels, and chambers of commerce. It helps to orient the visitor at the historic site; and it serves as a souvenir for those who want a memento of the trip.

Other interpretation methods can supplement or substitute for the human interpreter.—*Atlanta Historical Society, Inc.*

Ideally, historic sites should have separate leaflets for promotion and for orientation, but budgetary considerations seldom permit this. Thus, a single leaflet must often serve the combined purposes. As an aid to promotion, the leaflet must answer the prospective visitor's two primary questions: "Why should I want to see this site?" and "How do I get there?" As a means of orientation, the leaflet should explain the site's historical importance. As a souvenir, the leaflet should contain both historical information and illustrations of the physical appearance of the site. There should be a brief, factual text; pictorial elements showing the site; either a map or very clear directions on how to reach the site; and, for large areas, such as battlefields, or even very large building interiors, a map of the site itself.

Design must also be carefully considered. When folded, the leaflet must fit into standard leaflet display racks of hotels, restaurants, and travel agencies. This means that its maximum folded size must not exceed 4 by 9 inches. That size will also fit into a standard number ten envelope, so that the organization can use the leaflet in mail promotion; and it also fits nicely into purses and coat pockets.

These documents should be attractive—should have a "pick-me-up" appearance, attention-compelling enough to compete with other leaflets in the display rack. Color is essential. Two-color printing is not nearly so expensive as is commonly thought; but if stringent budgeting makes it impossible, comparable results can be obtained by using colored ink on colored paper. If one color of ink is used in the printing, that color should be dark, to gain maximum legibility. Dark inks are also better for photographic illustrations (halftones).

Generally speaking, it is a good idea to work with a professional designer in preparing a leaflet. The better printing companies have designers on their staffs. University and commercial presses also have designers, many of whom are willing to do outside work on a fee basis. A trained designer not only can help create an attractive layout for the text, illustrations, and map, but will be enormously helpful in selecting paper and inks for the job. Since his fee will usually be spread over a printing of ten thousand leaflets or more, the added cost per leaflet is quite small; and if the leaflet's added attractiveness encourages more people to visit the site, the investment will have been worthwhile. A word of caution should be entered, however, regarding the danger of design overwhelming text content. Remember that the leaflet must communicate, as well as be attractive.

One of the most common mistakes in the publishing of historic site leaflets is including too much information. The prospective visitor seldom needs a detailed history of the site to decide whether or not to visit it, and the person who is already on the premises, ready for the tour, will seldom delay to read a long text. Promotion and orientation are both served better by a short, concise text that gives the highlights of the history, and no more.

Booklet. The historical organization that wants to provide visitors with a detailed story of the site should consider publishing a separate booklet, supplementing the leaflet and serving different purposes. A booklet's primary purpose is education, rather than promotion and orientation. It has some souvenir value, though that is secondary. It is intended to be taken home and to give the visitor more information than there is space for on the leaflet and more than is likely to be included in human interpretations of the site.

A typical booklet for a documentary site will provide the site's history, an interpreted account of the historical events or persons that made it important, information about the people who have lived it, and perhaps an account of its acquisition and restoration. Some of the same information might be included for a representative or aesthetic site, but with other pertinent details. Booklet sizes vary, according to the amount of text and the use of illustrations. Typical page sizes are 5 by 8, 6 by 9, and 7 by 10 inches, and the number of pages usually will be sixteen or thirty-two, or occasionally sixty-four. (The number of pages has to be a multiple of four, and with most printers one gets the most pages for the money in multiples of sixteen, because of the way sheets are printed, folded, and stitched.) Booklets are more attractive if they are illustrated, and they may be printed in two colors of ink, though the latter is not necessary. The booklet's main purpose is to convey additional information in a publication attractive enough to reflect credit on the site and inexpensive enough to be well within the visitor's means, so that he will purchase it to satisfy his desire to know more about the site.

The quantity of booklets ordered will depend entirely on the site's volume of visitors, the number of questions customarily asked, and the judgment of the historical organization as to the document's potential sales. Prices usually start at two dollars. Print orders are seldom economical in quantities of less than 5,000, and sales are almost exclusively through the sales desk at the site.

Guidebook. Another category of publications is the guidebook. Its purpose is to tell the visitor what he is seeing, frequently with directions for the most effective route to take within the site. The guidebook is seldom used where human interpreters are available to conduct tours; it is basically a substitute for the human interpreter, and it enables the visitor to make a more informed, self-guided tour than otherwise would be possible.

The guidebook should provide a room-by-room (or, outdoors, a point-to-point) discussion of the history of the site and, as warranted, interpretation of the social significance of the furnishings to the house or its period. It should focus on the event or the site, however, not on age or provenance of the furnishings. It should tell the visitor what he is seeing and explain the site's importance.

The guidebook has a number of disadvantages as an interpretive device. If, in fact, it provides information the visitor really needs in order to understand what he is seeing, the document necessarily will have to be detailed. This means that it will be long, expensive to produce, and therefore costly for the visitor to purchase. The text has to be written on the assumption that the restoration is static and that all items of furniture or furnishings will be kept in the same place more or less permanently. Otherwise, the manual will have to be revised and reprinted at too frequent intervals. Guidebook descriptions must be written very clearly, but under no circumstances should references be numbered to correspond to prominent numbers affixed to the objects described. This practice happily has been abandoned in most places, but its memory lingers as an interpretive nightmare. Finally, the guidebook should not be used to memorialize the donors of the furnishings, to the boredom of the user and the interest of hardly anybody.

Guidebooks customarily are longer than historical booklets. They are seldom less than sixteen pages and are more likely to be thirty-two, forty-eight, or some other multiple of sixteen. Photographs, drawings, and maps or floor plans are essential. Every effort should be made to keep the cost low so that the expense of a visit is kept to a minimum. Thus, color printing will probably not be possible and binding will have to be inexpensive.

Catalogues. Catalogues are still another class of publications. They are similar to guidebooks in some respects, but they serve an essentially different purpose. More often created for aesthetic than for documentary or representative sites, catalogues are primarily intended to help the visitor learn about the objects on display and to serve the scholarly uses of persons making a study of those objects. Catalogues, therefore, are more closely identified with the collection than with the site's historic theme. They present detailed information on the objects displayed, telling when they were made, where, and by whom.

Catalogues are expected to be works of scholarship; and, like books, they are expected to reach a wider audience than the visitors who come to the site. Consequently, in content and in appearance, catalogues must compete with the offerings of other publishers in the field of the decorative arts. They are seldom less than sixty-four pages in length, and usually not less than one hundred. Illustrations are mandatory and should be of high quality. Catalogues are often found in hard covers, though a good-quality paper cover may be acceptable. The use of colored ink, or even of four-color process photographs, will depend on the funds available for printing. Print orders are likely to be small for most catalogues, and prices will be high as a consequence. Most sales will be at the site itself, but a limited market may be developed by mail.

Books. Books published by the site organization or purchased from other publishers for resale at the sales desk can be an important extension of the interpretive effort by helping the visitor pursue interests that have been aroused during the tour of the site. These offerings appropriately might include biographies of persons associated with the site, a history of the site itself, histories of the area or state in which the site is located, books that treat the general time period of the site, books dealing with the natural environment, books that help to explain things that went on at the site (handicrafts, agricultural pursuits, etc.), and children's books. Many of these books are available in paperback—and therefore inexpensive—editions from commercial and university presses.

Whether or not the site sells books will depend almost

entirely on available funds. The publication of a book requires a very large investment of capital that may require many years to recover through sales. If such an outlay is beyond the organization's means, consider the possibility of interesting a commercial or university publisher in the book. If the manuscript is scholarly, such a press might be willing to publish, if the site is willing to purchase enough books to assure the press that it will at least break even. This kind of arrangement not only makes publication possible, but gives the site organization the benefit of the professional editing, design, and marketing skills of the press.

Another way to develop a book sales program is to purchase from other presses books appropriate to the site. On most orders of three to five or more copies of the same book, one should expect to pay thirty-five to forty percent less than the established list price. Colonial Williamsburg and Old Sturbridge Village have developed substantial book sales through careful selection of titles and attractive display techniques. The ability of a site to parallel their success depends on the amount of visitation, available display and sales area, and whether the organization can tie up its funds until the books can be sold at a profit.

Museum Displays and Exhibits

Another commonly used interpretive device at historic sites is the museum display or exhibit. Properly used, the exhibit can be an important adjunct to the total interpretation effort. All too often, its potential is wasted, because many historical organizations fail to keep clearly in mind the basic objective of interpreting the historic site and decide that it would be "interesting" to display random historical objects that members of the community are willing to donate. At worst, the historic house becomes responsible for a collection of stuffed birds or ostrich eggs that have nothing to do with the location and, in fact, intrude upon the interpretation of the rest of the structure. Even if so jarring a note is avoided, it is equally undesirable to use outmoded department-store cases containing a collection of historical curiosities that tell us nothing about the people or the historical events associated with the site. They obscure and confuse the interpretation instead of helping it.

Good museum displays and exhibits, on the other hand, can help orient the visitor who has arrived at the site but has not started his tour, or they can enrich the visit by providing an extension of the tour. To do these things, the exhibits must include appropriate objects to help tell the historical story.

Placement. One of the main problems in creating museum displays at historic sites is where to put them. It is generally agreed that the best place is in a visitor center constructed for that purpose. The National Park Service and some state agencies have made extensive use of visitor centers to create what H. J. Swinney, Director Emeritus of the Strong Museum in Rochester, New York, has referred to as a giant label for the site. These centers usually contain interpretive exhibits plus auditorium, public rest rooms, sales desks, and administrative offices. Because such buildings are new, they can be designed for maximum security of the collections, proper lighting, and the meeting of generally accepted exhibit standards. If they are within the means of the historical organization, they are clearly the answer to a number of interpretive requirements.

Museum displays can also be installed in an acceptable outbuilding on the premises, provided such a structure is of fire-resistant construction or can be modified to provide adequate protection for the collections. Use of an outbuilding keeps the museum exhibits from intruding upon the historical atmosphere of the restored structure and makes it possible to light, display, and protect the collections in a proper manner without compromising the historical integrity of the main structure. If museum exhibits are to be in a separate building, however, the historical organization will have to have additional personnel to staff the museum building as well as the main structure.

Most historic sites have neither the funds for a visitor center, nor an outbuilding that they can develop into a secure museum area, nor the personnel with which to staff such a facility. Consequently, if museum exhibits are desired, they will have to be within the main historical building. This has several advan-

Visitor centers and orientation exhibits create "giant labels" for historic sites.—*Colonial Williamsburg Foundation*

tages and some notable disadvantages. On the plus side, the exhibit area may be the room in which the visitors wait for the beginning of the tour, perhaps in the same room in which admissions are paid and the sales desk is situated. Having the exhibit area in the main building makes it less likely that the visitor will miss seeing the exhibits, and additional personnel will not be required. On the minus side, the displays, no matter how effective, will be an intrusion in the old building. It is extremely difficult to provide effective lighting and use modern case design that will not clash with the historical period of the structure. It is also difficult to place the museum room so as to provide orientation and reception facilities and not have it affect the appearance of the main entrance to the building. Nevertheless, these difficulties have been surmounted by some sites in the past, and solutions are possible in the future.

Wherever the museum exhibits are located in the building, they will be a compromise between old and new, between the authenticity of the restoration and the demands of effective exhibit techniques. Perhaps the least compromising location is the basement of the structure, assuming that it is not of any great historical importance, but there are dangers in ascending and descending the stairs. A second possibility is a room that is not original to the historical structure, one that someday may be removed but in the meantime can be modernized for use as a museum. The third possibility is a room within the main part of the historical structure that is not needed for the main interpretation—a spare bedroom, for example, but one that has no great historical significance; or a servant's room, provided there is no likelihood that you will wish to use it to interpret the role of the servant of that period. Whatever the room, it should be of adequate size and adaptable for use as the museum. The historical organization must keep in mind that someday it or its successors may want to return the room to its historical appearance and move the museum exhibits to another place. Every effort should be made, therefore, to avoid structural changes that would require reconstruction at a later time. A skilled architect or exhibits designer can make major changes in the appearance of the room without disturbing the basic structure.

Assuming that the original structure can be preserved, there remains the decision whether to keep the room looking old or frankly to modernize it to fit its intended purpose. If the room is kept "old," it obviously will be easier to restore at some later date. The room's appearance will also be reasonably consistent with the rest of the house. But modern museum cases and lighting will assuredly clash with the old decor; and, besides, old houses, unless owned by eccentrics, didn't have museum rooms, so the illusion of "old" is destroyed, anyway. If the room is frankly modernized, it will be even more of an intrusion into the historical setting. Nevertheless, there is some merit in having a clear line of demarcation between the museum room and the restored structure. In the long run, the effectiveness of the museum displays as an interpretive device probably will benefit from the better facilities of the modern room. Both approaches are valid, however, each having its supporters and detractors.

Finally, some consideration must be given to the sequence in which exhibits are to be viewed as part of the over-all tour of the site. Are the exhibits to be seen at the beginning? If so, their primary purpose should probably be to prepare the visitor for the tour of the site. Do they come in the middle of the tour? Then how can they fit smoothly into the total interpretation, without being a distracting side road off the main highway? Or do the exhibits come at the end? Then they must supplement what has been seen, rather than repeat it.

One must also consider carefully how much to try to tell the visitor. Some of the earlier visitor centers of the National Park Service, for example, have been criticized for doing so thorough a job of preparing the visitor that he was worn out before he began the tour of the site. The more recent trend is to construct simpler (and less expensive) information centers for the starting point and to bring the visitor to the more elaborate and thorough centers at the end of the tour, trying there to answer many of the questions that may have arisen during the tour. This has been done very successfully at St. Marie-among-the-Hurons in Midland, Ontario.

The nature of the exhibits to be installed in the museum room must be determined by the objectives the organization has set for the site. The exhibits should supplement, extend, and clarify what one expects the visitor to learn and understand about the site. Obvious exhibit topics are the event that made the site famous, information about the people who once lived in the building and what they were like, the story of the restoration itself (stressing what was done and how, *not who* did it), or what meaning the site, its event, or its inhabitants have for the person of today. Once a theme has been selected, objects, historical photographs, maps, broadsides, and similar graphics should be chosen to illustrate the theme. These should not be displayed for their own sake but for the sake of the understanding they will contribute to the viewer of the well-planned exhibit. They must also be properly labelled with short, concise printed text or audio tapes. Remember that what "everybody" knows locally about the structure is not what everybody knows who comes to the site. In planning the exhibit, remember the old adage that one should never overestimate the knowledge of the visitor nor underestimate his intelligence.

One additional kind of exhibit ought to be mentioned, and that is the wayside exhibit. When the visitor must tour over a sizeable area, such as a battlefield or the spacious grounds of a large estate, the wayside exhibit can be very helpful in orienting him during the tour and helping him to understand the significance of what he is seeing. Wayside exhibits, because they are not under continuous scrutiny of the staff, seldom contain original artifacts. Replicas may sometimes be employed, but they invite vandalism from the undiscerning thief. Customarily, the wayside exhibit contains copies of historical graphic materials along with printed labels. Sometimes it also has an audio label or interpretation, but the problem of vandalism limits extensive use of this procedure.

The techniques for creating good museum and wayside exhibits are beyond the scope of this book. The list of selected readings contains a number of titles that are extremely useful, all of them available from the American Association for State and Local History. Special attention should be called to Arminta Neal's *Exhibits for the Small Museum*, which is an invaluable aid to all museum exhibit planners and designers. And, as in printing, the professional exhibit designer is often more than worth his fee.

Audio Devices

In recent years the tremendous strides in the field of recorded sound have opened up new dimensions for the interpreter. Not only can oral history programs provide additional information for the interpreter to use in his presentation, but tape recordings can be utilized to supplement the human interpreter's efforts or, in some instances, to replace him. Increasing public acceptance of recorded sound as a tool of learning is attested by the number of students carrying tape recorders to classroom and seminars and by the reliance of a disproportionate part of the population upon the spoken word, rather than the written word, as a source of knowledge. We may deplore the generation of listeners—and

Exhibits can be an important part of the interpretation, interpreting sites where human interpreters are not practical. —*Plimoth Plantation*

nonreaders—but the interpreter will do well to utilize the media to which his audience is accustomed.

Audio devices can be employed in a variety of ways in the interpretation of historic sites. They can, for example, provide explanations of objects, rooms, or places without a human interpreter being present. The button to push or the listening device to lift to the ear are familiar to most historic site visitors. Audio tapes can provide appropriate background sounds or music appropriate to the interpretation, as with some of the very effective exhibits at the Milwaukee County Museum. They can also add a touch of realism to the visit, as at the Franklin D. Roosevelt home, Hyde Park, where one's interpreter, part of the time, is the late Mrs. Roosevelt; or at the Truman Library of Independence, Missouri, where one can view a reproduction of the White House Oval Office while listening to the late President Harry S. Truman discuss his presidential responsibilities.

One of the most important potential uses of audio interpretation is for battlefields, where the continuity of the story is difficult to maintain from site to site within the larger area. These battlefields present special problems because of their size and the necessary limitation in the number of guides that can be hired to present them. As Frank Barnes, former Chief of Interpretation for the Northeast Region of the National Park Service, has said, the tape tour, if done well, "does usually *assure a well-done, well-thought-out tour every time.*" The biggest problem of such a tour has been that the visitor has no opportunity to ask questions, but some sites provide telephones so that visitors can talk directly to an interpreter.

With the increased miniaturization of electronic components, it has become much easier to hide audio devices where they are needed. A tiny button in the woodwork can activate a hidden speaker in the historical room. The same can be done at a museum case exhibit. Audio equipment can also be located in outdoor spots where a narration is wanted, as at a number of National Park Service installations. Portable cassette tape players can be used in automobiles, and considerable progress has been made toward the use of controlled short-range transmitters which beam messages that can be picked up by passing automobile radios.

Audio systems, by eliminating the need for human interpreters where their use is too expensive or impractical, have made interpretation available where it formerly was almost impossible. Moreover, the attention span for a good audio presentation appears to be greater than for a written label, an advantage interpreters have exploited to increase the amount of information they are providing. Audio systems have other advantages for role-playing interpretation and in situations where sound effects can enhance the realism of the mood sought by the interpreter.

These advantages are balanced against some important shortcomings, of which the biggest is the problem of maintenance of the equipment. Spare machines must be on hand to replace those that malfunction, thus increasing the cost of the audio installation. Tapes break and snarl frequently, causing a percentage of all visitors to leave without the intended message—

unless, that is, audio labels are supplemented with written ones. Some systems require the visitor to wear uncomfortable earphones that intrude on the pleasure of the visit. Earphones also must be sanitized between uses. The theft problem for outdoor tape repeaters is a major handicap, so much so that one site in a western state finally hid the repeater in a brush-covered underground installation and constructed nearby a dummy enclosure that is designed to frustrate and delay would-be thieves. Finally, many organizations use the devices to excess, not only taping messages that are too long but relying so heavily on taped interpretation that the visitor cannot ask questions.

Excepting when the audio device is used to guide the visitor on a tour, its primary application is as a spoken label. The same rules apply to audio labels as to those that are written. They need to be brief enough not to exceed the attention span of the listener, though customarily good audio does not have to be as brief as a good written label. Like the written label, the audio message must be clear and understandable to the visitor. Generally speaking, therefore, it is best to record the audio message with the voice of a person who has had theatrical or announcer training. Heavy accents should be avoided, since they may be unintelligible to persons from other sections of the country. Voices of real historical personages may be used, provided they will be understood readily by the visitor. Don't overlook the possibilities of using good historical voices; the proliferation of oral history programs means there are on tape many voices that might be able to add to the realism of your interpretation.

Don't overlook, either, the possibility of creating a more dramatic audio interpretation through spoken role-playing. This can be insufferably bad, if poorly done, but it can be extremely effective if done well. The authentic atmosphere created by the good performance can have almost as much impact as the real voice of the historical figure.

Audiovisual Interpretation

Interpretation that combines both sound and visual images has an impact that usually surpasses that of an audio recording alone. It also has a bigger price tag. The number of possibilities for combining sound and images is enormous, ranging from the narrated slide lecture to elaborate sound-and-light dramatic productions. For our purposes we shall restrict our discussion to various combinations of sound with still photography and motion pictures.

In the interpretation of historic sites, the audiovisual production serves a number of purposes. It is a highly successful device for the interpretive orientation of the visitor, as has been demonstrated at numerous National Park Service Visitor Centers. It can interpret topics that cannot be handled by most human interpreters, motion picture films and video tapes, for example, can show the techniques of crafts so specialized that only a few people in the country can perform them. Audiovisual productions can also extend the educational program of the historic site into the community or across the nation. National Park Service films, for example, have extended interpretations of many sites to people who may never see them any other way. Finally, audiovisual devices of various sorts can serve as functional parts of exhibits that are part of the interpretive program.

Recent technological advances have made the videocassette recorder and television monitor an increasingly affordable medium. Such units are relatively trouble-free, the tapes are inexpensive to reproduce, and the picture entirely suitable for small groups of people. Within a few years, large screens may make it possible to employ video for much larger groups. Video also has the advantages of providing images suitable for viewing in normal room light and without the intrusive sounds of mechanical projection equipment.

For larger audiences, the most common of audiovisual presentations is motion picture or slide projection. The old crystal-beaded screen may be used where light is relatively subdued, but newer lenticular screens provide a more brilliant picture and tolerate more room light without diminishing quality. The angle from which the image can be viewed is smaller with the lenticular screen, however, than with the beaded. For visitor comfort, viewing rooms for either motion pictures or slides should not contain the projector. The projector noise is obtrusive, and can readily be muffled by constructing a separate projection booth to shut the sound off from the audience. Such a booth also eliminates the potential accident of a visitor tripping over the maze of electrical wires needed to run the system.

Tape-slide shows. The most economical audiovisual production for most sites will be the tape-slide show. This kind of show can be produced by amateurs, though they should be advanced in technique and capable of producing both pictures and sound of professional quality. Equipment costs are reasonable: for an investment of $1,100 (exclusive of camera), a cassette tape recorder-slide projector combination can be purchased in which the cassette not only plays the sound but also, by means of recorded but inaudible sound impulses, actuates the slide-changing mechanism. The tape-slide show can be started by a staff member and be playing during his absence from the room. This kind of show also has an enormous advantage over other audiovisual productions in terms of flexibility. New tapes can be made with minimal effort; new slides can be inserted at any time in order to bring the show up to date.

Obviously, the tape-slide show has its shortcomings. Still pictures, unless very skillfully used, are not very effective in showing action. Much of the equipment used in these productions is of fairly recent design and is changing rapidly, so obsolescence and service may be problems. Tape-slide shows are also difficult to send out for use by other groups. The cassette-projector combination is not uncommon, but neither is it readily available. Experienced operators are scarce, and in the hands of inexperienced projectionists slides and tapes may be damaged.

Filmstrips. The filmstrip need concern us only briefly. So far as the combination of sound and pictures is concerned, the show seen by the audience is virtually indistinguishable from the tape-slide show. In the film-strip show, the sound is synchronized with the projection of a series of photographic images that appear in sequence on a continuous strip of film— thus the name. The film-strip medium is used primarily where there is a substantial market for multiple copies of the show.

Filmstrip equipment is available in many schools, which use it in their instructional program. For audiovisual programs that may need extensive duplication, the filmstrip is probably the answer, even though it requires a greater beginning investment to produce the master film from which future filmstrips will be made. When there is a need only for one or two still-picture programs, the tape-slide show will probably prove more useful.

Multiple-projector tape-slide. If the historic site wants to advance to a still more sophisticated audiovisual presentation utilizing still pictures, it can go to a multiple-projector tape-slide show. In its simplest form, this process uses two slide projectors precisely focused on the same area of the screen and controlled by a dissolve unit. The dissolve unit causes the slides to be projected alternately by the two projectors, with one image slowly fading, or dissolving, as the other image takes over the screen. This does away with the abrupt intervals of blackened screen between slides and makes for more pleasant viewing. It also requires at least a semipermanent projection room somewhere at the site.

For those with still more sophisticated tastes, the multiple-projector system with its dissolve unit can be multiplied to what is called a multiscreen system in which two, three, or more pictures are projected at the same time by as many multiprojector units. What may sound at first like total chaos can be very effective, as in the orientation show at the Lahaina Restoration on the Island of Maui in Hawaii. The multiscreen presentation is particularly effective when one wishes to show an extreme close-up next to an ordinary view of an object or simultaneously to show a historical and a present-day view of the same subject. But the technique tends to be gimmicky unless done with great sensitivity. And even then, the equipment maintenance is difficult and may require a trained audio-visual technician as operator.

Motion picture film. The motion picture film (and its close cousin, the videotape) is the ultimate in the audiovisual field. Most visitors to the historic site are oriented to the medium of film because of their exposure to Hollywood productions and television programs. Motion pictures can be reproduced in multiple copies for widespread distribution, and a good film can be used on television. Equipment for showing motion pictures is generally available. Like the tape-slide show, a film can be started by a staff member who can then leave until the show is finished.

The biggest disadvantage of the motion picture is its expense. At current prices, the cost to produce a good motion picture is estimated at $3,000 per minute. A motion picture is also an inflexible package when portions of it become outdated or outmoded. It is extremely difficult to film a new scene to replace one that has become obsolete. The motion picture also depends on noisy equipment that is even more distracting than that used in tape-slide shows when operated in small rooms. In addition, one must expect film damage at the hands of unskillful projectionists and be prepared to pay the costs of film inspection and cleaning and of replacement footage. The problem of maintaining motion-picture projection equipment is, of course, shared with the rest of the audiovisual media.

Detailed information on the production of motion pictures is beyond the scope of this book. Motion pictures are too complex and are clearly the job of professional film makers, not of historic site organizations, which should approach this aspect of interpretation very cautiously and seek lots of expert advice to be sure of getting a quality product and a fair price.

Audiovisual interpretation, in summary, can be enormously helpful to the historic site. In a television-conditioned society, motion pictures, videotapes, and tape-slide shows are an accustomed means of learning, for people will watch, though they may not read. But there are dangers. One can rely on AV too much as a substitute for doing effective work with the *real* objects which, after all, are what mainly distinguish historic sites from their amusement-park copies. There is the additional danger of aesthetic or design considerations overwhelming the historical message, simply because the technicalities of the audiovisual field are beyond the comprehension of most historians. Even so, the dangers and the shortcomings are outweighed by the effectiveness that audiovisual interpretation can provide for a growing historic site audience.

The extent to which printed materials, museum case exhibits, and audiovisual productions should substitute for, or supplement, human interpretation depends on a number of considerations. Foremost among these, of course, is the simple question of what is needed to interpret the site to the public with greatest effectiveness.

Many concepts and facts are not easily understood through a spoken interpretation. Consider, for example, how difficult it would be to understand the geological formation of the Grand Canyon through a spoken interpretation, even if you were looking at the canyon at the same time the interpreter was talking. A motion picture or tape-slide show is almost essential in such an instance. Or consider the interpretation of the Valley Forge encampment. Is it likely that a Southern Californian, seeing the site in August, will perceive very clearly the suffering of the Revolutionary troops in their bitterly cold winter quarters? A pictorial interpretation could at least communicate a visual image of snow; and a museum case exhibit of the troops' inadequate clothing, presented in a walk-in refrigerator, would certainly exceed all but the most effective verbal presentations. And finally, the learning process will almost always be furthered if there are suitable printed materials for the visitors to take home.

A second consideration is coping with the physical characteristics of the site itself. If there are widely scattered outbuildings, it may be impossible to staff them and equally impossible to interpret them adequately from the structures that are staffed. Under these circumstances, message repeaters, or carefully composed labels, or a well-designed permanent exhibit may be important adjuncts of the main interpretive effort. Even if the site consists of only one building, the limited size of the interpretive staff may dictate the use of message repeaters or appropriate labels. This will be true when there are no guided tours, or when tours are limited to the ground floor, with the remaining rooms open for self-guided visits.

A third consideration is the desire of some sites to insure that virtually every visitor receives a very precise and uniform presentation of facts and concepts either as the whole interpreta-

Museum lighting and display techniques increase the effectiveness of interpretive exhibits.—*The Margaret Woodbury Strong Museum*

tion or as a portion of the whole. An orientation film is a good example of this. It tells things that would otherwise have to be presented by the interpreters. More important, by its being presented at the beginning of the visit, the interpreters are able to assume a common, basic knowledge of the site on the part of members of each tour group. A thoughtfully prepared audio or audiovisual presentation can also be useful in presenting information of a potentially controversial nature. During some of the more heated periods of civil rights controversy in the 1960s, for example, several sites tried to insure a balanced and sensitive interpretation of black history by removing that topic from the human interpretation, and presenting it, instead, through message repeaters and motion pictures. Some interpretations of religious history are also presented in this way, for the same reasons.

Finally, of course, there is the consideration of financial capability. Even though publications, museum exhibits, and audiovisual programs need not be terribly expensive, they are almost never free. And most historic site organizations, given a choice between investing in better interpretation or saving for the next roof repair or painting job, are likely to give priority to the physical structure. Obviously, there will be nothing to interpret if the site is not properly maintained; but without effective interpretation, there will be neither the informed visitor who is the ultimate objective of the restoration nor the pleased visitor who is the most important single key to future visitation—and to future revenues.

6

Interpreting for School Tours

SOME historic site organizations view the arrival of a bright yellow school bus and its tour-group cargo with consternation. More progressive sites view these organized student groups as both a challenge and an opportunity. The challenge is to help young, flexible minds understand and develop an appreciation for the past. The opportunity is to make these children a positive factor in encouraging greater visitation to the site and in providing future support for the historic preservation movement when they become voting adults.

There is a growing trend in education to get the class out of the classroom and to provide concrete, tangible, on-site evidence of the stuff books are made of. Schools are using all sorts of community resources as a vital part of today's education. Educators agree that education and museums need each other. They also agree that organized groups of students require special treatment if they are to gain any understanding from their visit. Although full of physical energy, children tire quickly unless their interest is sustained at a high level. Although capable of understanding far more than their parents would have at the same age—as any parent will testify—their attention span is relatively short. Although many are full of curiosity, they are likely to be disconcerting to the tour guide because their curiosity is much more open than that of adults; they ask questions without the self-consciousness that an adult feels when he fears he will appear stupid or uninformed. But interest level and reactions vary enormously, from very strong interest and vital questions, through real or feigned boredom to occasional rudeness and poor behavior. All levels of interest must be cared for as well as possible.

Very few historic sites have the staff and money with which to set up elaborate school group programs, with special buildings and separate staff. Most sites can establish some kind of program, however, and there are important inducements to do so. One is obtaining better control over the time when school tours will arrive at the site. Another is being able to make the visit a more significant experience for the children and therefore more worthwhile in terms of time the interpreters spend with the tour group. Still a third is being able to view the departing bus as a group of converts who will bring parents and friends on return visits.

In establishing schedules for special tours, the site organization should consider not only the times when it is most convenient for school groups to make the tour, but also when those times will coincide with classroom instruction. The site organization may also wish to schedule student groups during slack periods of regular visitation. This usually means having no scheduled tours on weekends, during Easter or spring holidays, or at times when it is likely to be especially difficult to provide special guides for the tours.

If the site is prepared to go to even greater lengths to improve its school-group interpretation and encourage advance appointments, it may offer to send instructional material in advance, so that the children and the teacher can have an orientation before their arrival. Some sites have gone beyond this and prepared special tape-slide or filmstrip shows that the teacher can use in preparing the class for the visit. A few sites even send kits of museum objects, either originals or replicas, that may be examined and handled by the children in their classrooms before the visit.

Separating children and adults. As a rule, school groups should be kept separated from adult visitors for maximum benefit to both groups. A few of the larger historic sites do this to some extent. In these places, the school groups and the adult visitors are not competing with each other for a view of certain areas. At most historic sites, however, this separation of school groups from adult visitors is more difficult. Whenever possible, the administration should develop special procedures which

Many historic sites now handle school programs. Above, a volunteer conducts a group of students separately from the adult visitors.— *Oregon Historical Society; photograph by George Champlin*

will work school groups in between adult groups with as little mixing as possible.

It is important that neither the school groups nor adult groups be pushed aside. The interpreter should explain to visitors why their group has to wait briefly. The interpreter should also use the waiting time to talk about interesting details that, but for the delay, could not have been covered. This is also a good time for questions and answers, and for finding out something about site visitors—who they are, where they are from, and their interests.

Conducting school groups. The following procedures may be helpful in distributing school groups around a large historic area such as a National Park, and in keeping them under control:

1. Whenever possible, the staff person in charge of school tours should assign school groups to different starting points

Visits by large school groups should be timed for the convenience of both the group and the site. Here, a docent points out features of a "Fire Lily" quilt.—*Ohio Historical Society*

around the historic area in order to avoid having at one particular location more groups than can be handled at the same time.

2. When a number of school groups are expected to arrive at one area at the same time, the person in charge of the area should work the school groups in between the regular adult groups on an equitable basis. The school group should not be pushed aside indefinitely or conveniently forgotten just because "they are children."

3. The adults accompanying the school groups should remain with them at all times, unless the historic site interpreters instruct them otherwise.

4. Interpreters conducting adult groups as well as those conducting school groups should be conscious of the need to shorten interpretations during busy times and to move groups along as quickly as possible so that no group is held up longer than absolutely necessary.

5. Sometimes, despite the best efforts to hold interest, one encounters an unruly school group that disturbs adult groups or even other school groups, and who might actually cause damage to furnishings. Such a group should be taken out of a building immediately and—as unobtrusively as possible— returned to the starting point, and they should not be allowed to continue the tour. Such an incident should be reported to the director of the site. If it is known ahead of time that a school group is unruly, they should not be permitted to enter the site at all.

It will also help to control school groups if certain instructions are spelled out in advance and sent to those in charge of arranging for a school tour. For example:

1. Where the group should park their bus or cars.
2. Where they should enter the building
3. How to arrange a restroom stop *before* the tour
4. What areas those of certain grade levels should cover and which they should bypass
5. Where and when the group will eat lunch
6. Where the interpreter conducting the group should take them first, and in what order for the rest of the tour.

7. What emphasis should be made for particular grade levels.

There is another important element of control that should be mentioned. The historic site organization should not feel obligated to provide free baby-sitting service so the teacher can have part of a day free of responsibility. It may, like Old Economy, choose to exclude adults except for staff, but many sites find it helpful to require that there be one adult for every ten or fifteen students, and further to require that the adults must be with the tour group at all times during the visit. It should be clearly understood that these adults are responsible for the conduct of the children. The potential damage to irreplaceable objects is too great to risk having an unruly tour group unaccompanied by persons who have the authority to assist the guide in maintaining order.

Finally, in the same vein, the site should establish realistic limits on the size of the school groups taken on the tour. For most sites, it is advisable to limit any one group to not more than twenty to twenty-five children. If the bus tour brings more students than that, they should be divided into two or more groups, both for control and to provide the best possible interpretation.

Developing the interpretation for children. Many historic site organizations assume that the interpretation they give to school groups should be essentially the same as that given adults, only "watered down." They simplify the standard interpretation to adapt it to the level of learning they think they might have attained at the same age. But the chances are that they do not remember correctly how much they knew at age ten or twelve; and even if they did, it has little bearing on what the youngster of today knows. Moreover, the interpreter—unless well-informed about current approaches to teaching—is likely to assume that the children will respond well to the pedagogical techniques of one or two generations ago. That would also be a mistake.

There is a need to develop over-all objectives for interpreting to students. Historic site organizations must decide what is attainable immediately, what can be developed as a part of long-range plans, and what personnel are available with the needed information and skills to plan special programs for school children. The organization might well consider using graduate students who are looking for projects for course credit at a nearby college, regularly employed teachers willing to undertake such a project during the summer months, or retired teachers who might be interested in using their long experience in the classroom to help prepare historic site programs for children.

The first step toward the development of interpretive techniques for school groups is to recognize the children's need to participate in the interpretation. While the adult may be content to view things and be told about them, the child's curiosity and restlessness is expressed in the urge to touch, feel, and handle objects, and particularly to make them work. It is in this area that the historic site can make a major contribution to their education. Sites have original and authentic objects as well as location in original and authentic places. In a world full of copies and disposable things, sites have genuine artifacts and real buildings and outdoor areas, used a long time ago, that can be seen, and walked through, and some of them even handled. Old Sturbridge Village, for example, has created an elaborate learning center in which tour children pitch hay, flail and winnow wheat, and use small implements that were part of early nineteenth-century town and farm life in New England. Colonial Williamsburg uses one of its restored original houses for school groups, where they can handle many eighteenth-century objects and participate in activities common to eighteenth-century home life.

Keeping in mind children's innate desire to touch, feel, and use real objects, the site organization should consider how to communicate its story to the children. Some sites employ the more or less conventional tour-lecture approach with some success. Others argue that the presentation should be a give-and-take discussion. Still others try to stimulate inductive reasoning through the inquiry method. Some even create special projects, both written and unwritten, that are to be done either as part of the tour or in preparation for it. There are probably as many "best" methods of interpreting for children as there are directors for such interpretation, and clearly the approach that is most successful with one interpreter may fail utterly if tried

At the 1900 Farm, students have a "hands-on" meeting with a draft horse. — *Iowa Living History Farms; photograph by Miriam Dunlap*

by another interpreter with different personality and training. The important thing is to recognize that there are a number of methods of interpreting to children, that you ought to be at least passingly familiar with those methods, and that you should employ whatever methods best suit your interpreter staff and provide the best possible tour for the school group.

The next step of the interpretive program should be to determine how the site and its objects can best be related to the programs of the schools from which the tours are coming. This means seeking the help of the teachers of social studies. Usually, school tours are made in connection with particular teaching units being studied by the children. Therefore, interpreters need to know what kinds of information the children are given within those teaching units; what related information or facts they can be expected to know when they make their visit to the

An interpreter encourages students to experience an exhibit through the sense of touch.—*Oregon Historical Society; photograph by George Champlin*

site; and what kinds of concepts—as distinguished from facts—the teachers are dealing with at this grade level. With the teacher's help, the interpreter can then perceive how the historic site might help to illustrate or illuminate or extend the children's understanding of the information or concepts they have been studying.

It should be noted, in passing, that a site organization may well decide to pursue a somewhat different set of interpretive objectives for its school groups than it does for its regular visitors. For example, a teacher may wish to visit a documentary site primarily for what it typifies about the social or economic order of a particular era instead of for the event or person connected with it. Within the limits of historical truth, the site should be agreeable to this approach, confident in the knowledge that members of a successful tour group will likely return again to receive the interpretation that the site organization wants them to have.

It is instructive to see how a historic site develops an effective children's tour program. Old Economy Village, in Pennsylvania, developed one of the outstanding programs of its kind, and the way in which it was planned has been described by Patricia Black Reibel:

> During the development of Old Economy's education program, we have designed three different programs. The first program coincides with the introduction to formal education at the kindergarten level. It combines an introduction to the past with an old-fashioned Christmas celebration. The second program, "Adventures in Wool," is for the second- or third-grade level—depending upon the school district. Some introduce the concept of community at the second- and some at the third-grade level. The third program, the "Everyday Life" tour, is presented for the fourth, fifth, or sixth grades—again depending upon when the pioneer unit is presented in the curriculum. "Everyday Life" emphasizes living in an 1820-1830 village. All school systems seem to have a unit which we call "Westward Ho," usually in the fifth, but sometimes in the fourth or sixth grades.[1]

Mrs. Reibel maintains that the historic site staff must be primarily responsible for the development of its own material:

1. Patricia F. Black, *The Live-In at Old Economy* (Ambridge, Pennsylvania: The Harmonie Associates, 1972), pp. 5-6.

One method of involving children on a personal level is to facilitate comparison of their lives with the lives of those who lived at the site.—
Sleepy Hollow Restorations

The historic site staff person (paid or volunteer) in charge of researching the school program contacts several schools in the area and asks to borrow the set of social studies curriculum used in the school. There are a variety of curricula in use which is why several schools are contacted.

The museum staff or a committee of volunteers should read the various curricula. The resources of the site should be evaluated to determine what the site has to offer to supplement the work done in the classroom.

The museum staff or committee of volunteers should begin development of an initial program. The beginnings may be small and hesitant, but the programs will grow as the newly formed education department gains confidence and experience.[2]

Developing Tours to Appeal to School Children's Give-and-Take Discussions

To achieve tours that will interest children, one cannot adopt the "children should be seen but not heard" attitude. Children need to be personally involved in the interpretation. One way of doing this is to compare their lives with the lives of people who lived at the site. Another way is to ask questions of them that give them a chance to guess what the answer might be. For example, suppose you were trying to help a group of fifth-grade children understand what education was like at the Sam Houston Schoolhouse, near Maryville, Tennessee, in the early nineteenth century. You might say something like this:

> You boys and girls are in the fifth grade, I understand. That means you are about ten or eleven. Right? Well, if you had lived in this area when Sam Houston taught at this school, you would have been expected to arrive here about half an hour after sunrise. Do you know why it wasn't, say, at 7:30? No? Well, many homes didn't have a watch or clock. So their days were governed by when the sun rose and when it set.
>
> How do you suppose the children got to school? Right, there was no school bus. Well, there may have been a few who rode horses. But most of them walked, even if it was cold and

2. Patricia B. Reibel to W. T. Alderson, August 26, 1974.

raining. How would you like to walk two or three miles to school in the rain? And then the same distance back home?

You know, another difference between then and now is that they didn't go to school as many years as you do. Farming was hard work and children were needed to help do that work. Can you guess why these children had a vacation in the fall, each year? That's right. What kind of farm work would they have done then? Right. Harvesting the crops. And most of them ended their schooling when they were a year or two older than you boys and girls. From then on, their learning depended on the reading they did at home.

The technique used here is to teach children something about what it would have been like to live in this particular place nearly two hundred years ago by asking questions that lead to their making comparisons and imagining themselves in that period of time, or by using anecdotes to make the story more interesting. This type of involvement of children in the interpretation does not require special equipment. You use what you have; you do not just lecture; you involve children through questions and answers.

Even more complicated subjects such as representative government can be explained to young children by making comparisons with their own experience, by asking questions in give-and-take discussion, rather than solely by lecturing. For example:

Do you know what representative government means? Do you have a student council in your school? If you have, you know that each class elects one or two students to represent them in the student council. What does your student council do? Yes, they make plans for school activities, sometimes draw up rules for behavior in school, and help teachers in any way they can. That is representative government. What do you suppose would happen if your entire school tried to get together at one time to work out school problems? It might be difficult, with so many students! But when you have students whom you have elected to represent you, you can know that your interests are being taken care of. If they aren't, what can you do? That's right, you can vote them out of office the next time!

If there is no student council in the school, the following approach may help students to understand representative government:

When your parents vote for the president of the United States, a member of Congress, a governor, or a city council-man, they are voting for someone to represent them in government. Could all the people in this country go to Washington or to the state capital or even to city hall? That would be a lot of people, wouldn't it? Instead, we send representatives to run the government.

Inductive Method of Interpretation

One of the most valuable techniques of interpretation is the use of the inductive method. The term *inductive method* has the sound of professional jargon, but it need not be intimidating. It is simply a method of arriving at truth by observing many particular facts and drawing general truths from them. It is the opposite of the *deductive method*, which begins with general truths and reasons from them what the particulars should be. In the deductive method, for example, we rely more on the authority of others: for example, electric lighting and wiring in homes began after Edison's invention of the incandescent bulb in 1879; a historic house built in 1870, therefore, couldn't have had an electric washing machine. In the inductive method, we rely more on our own observations to reach the conclusion: the house has no evidence of wiring, lights, or any kind of electric appliances; it does, however, have a big tub in a room adjacent to the kitchen area, and that room has hooks on the wall that might have held clotheslines; therefore, we can conclude that they did not have an electric washing machine and that they probably washed clothing by hand.

The interpreter encourages the visiting child to use inductive reasoning by using a method of inquiry that directs the child's attention to certain physical characteristics of the site or its surroundings. The child may then draw conclusions that reveal to him a segment of the truth about the past for that particular site. The following example of an interpretation of a historical kitchen helps to demonstrate the method.

Now, are all of you in the door? Fine.

This is the kitchen. It has been restored to its appearance in 1890. Now, let's see what we can learn from this kitchen about the differences in the way people lived then and now. Look around for a few minutes and then we'll discuss it.

. . .

All right, now that you've had time to examine the room, who wants to start? Dorothy does. That's right, Dorothy, there's no refrigerator. What else can we observe about food storage, back then? No freezer, either. Now, what difference would that make in what people ate? Jim says that things we eat today that have to be kept cold would not have been in their diet. Do you all agree? Barbara has a question. Yes, Barbara, that's an icebox. The block of ice went up here. All right, Barbara, how does this change our idea about their food? Right! They could keep things cool, but not frozen. So fruit juice, meat, and vegetables that we get frozen would have been stored in some other form. Yes, they had canned foods that they bought, and they canned a lot themselves.

Now, what about preparing foods? Yes, that's the stove. Yes, that's the woodbox beside it. You're right, Jim. Cooking was harder for the housewife, having to handle that heavy wood. It was also harder for children your age, who had to learn to split kindling and bring wood in to keep the box full.

Yes! The thing that's shaped like an iron, there on the stove, *is* an iron. That's right, Donny, it had to be heated on the stove. . . ."

As Richard H. Brown has written. "To ask questions of history is to learn a mode of inquiry which can be carried outside the classroom and which will be serviceable for a lifetime. . . . It is to learn what a fact is, how one comes by it, and most importantly of all, how one uses it."[3]

3. Richard H. Brown, "A Note to Teachers," in Allan A. Knownslar and Donald D. Frizzle, *Discovering American History* (New York: Holt, Rinehart, and Winston, 1970), p. xvi.

Role-Playing for Children

Almost every person can recall the fun he had as a child, pretending to be someone else—playing house and assuming the role of the father of the family, with the authority to direct the household; or mothering the "baby" in the form of one's favorite doll; shooting it out as cowboys and Indians in a dramatic battle involving play guns and attacks from hiding places; examining the "patient" with stethoscope around the neck and miniature doctor's bag handy; dressing up in mama's old dress and cast-off shoes and becoming a fine lady for a few hours. These and similar pastimes have enchanted children from the beginning of time. The children are removed temporarily from their own lives and are recreated in assumed roles which stimulate their imaginations and for the time being become "reality."

A number of historic sties have taken advantage of this penchant for role-playing to develop special programs that give children an opportunity to relive some specific period of history. History comes alive for them, because they are a part of it.

Partial role-playing is accomplished at some museums through the simple device of letting children wear a coonskin cap or an old-fashioned ladies' bonnet, handle a Kentucky rifle, run a hand over an unsheared sheep, or bounce about on a straw mattress on an old-style bed. Even if only one child out of a group is allowed to handle an object or perform a task common to a past era, the entire class seems to have a feeling of involvement. Their imaginations are stimulated.

Barnes Riznik, Director of Grove Farm and former Director of Education at Old Sturbridge Village, maintains that children learn more at a historic site than in school about family life of a hundred or a hundred and fifty years ago. He emphasizes the need for a pre-field-trip study at the site for teachers and a follow-up evaluation study in the classroom if a school visit is to be successful.

At Old Sturbridge Village, children are allowed to do many of the things their nineteenth-century counterparts would have done in the towns and farms of New England. In addition, Sturbridge Village has a special two-week summer program in

A young visitor plays "dress up" in period costume.—*Winterthur Museum and Gardens*

which children are dressed in nineteenth-century costumes and participate in very nearly every activity that a citizen of a small New England village or farm community would have experienced in earning his living, entertaining himself, maintaining a household, attending religious services, being educated, and taking part in local government. For example, after being briefed on the issues involved in a proposal for building a mill within the town limits, a group of children may participate in a town meeting characteristic of New England towns in the nineteenth century. The children take turns speaking for or against the proposal in a democratic way and then vote on whether the mill should be permitted. This experience gives children a concept of the basic principles of a government in which the people have a right to be heard. Reading about such a process would never mean as much as playing the role of a nineteenth-century citizen.

Another form of role-playing has been used at Old Economy Village. It is a day-long "Live-In," designed to help children understand what it would have been like to live in a small village founded by a group of Harmonists in 1824 for the practice of their religion. Old Economy staff personnel have discovered that fifth graders respond to the experience better than either younger or older children. They also have found that it is best to limit the size of the group to six boys and six girls, and to choose children for the "live-in" by lot rather than to allow the teacher to select only the brightest, best-behaved youngsters. One thrilled little boy exclaimed, "I am so glad that our teacher let us draw straws to see who could come. She never would have chosen me, because she thinks I don't work very hard on my school work."

When the children arrive at 8:30 A.M. for the Live-In experience, parents and teachers are sent on their way, to return at 3:00 P.M. to pick up the chosen few. The staff discovered, during their first year of experimenting with the Live-In, that teachers and parents, when allowed to accompany the groups, tended to disrupt the atmosphere the staff was trying to create.

As soon as the children arrive, they are fitted with costumes. The girls have been asked to wear long skirts, if they have them,

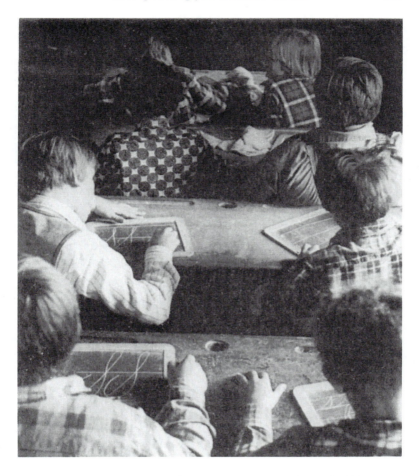

Writing on slates is one task for the students spending a half-day in a re-created 1875 schoolroom.—*Iowa Living History Farms; photograph by Miriam Dunlap*

and they are now given bonnets and aprons that are copied from original Harmonist wearing apparel. The boys are fitted with the type of work aprons men wore in the 1830s, and with wide-brimmed black hats. One can see the youngsters already beginning to live the life of the past when they put on the costumes. Then they are given a brief introduction about the Harmonist Society and told that they are going to become Brothers and Sisters in a Harmonist household, performing the chores that they would have performed, had they lived there back in the early nineteenth century.

Patricia Black Reibel, who once directed the program, says:

> The Live-In is designed to illustrate a day in the life of a child in 1830. . . . Youngsters simply cannot imagine how people lived without the telephone, television, and running water—or even without paper bags and cardboard boxes. . . . Instead of running water, the Live-In features "running" boys with a yoke and two buckets, fetching water from the pump. A turn of a knob now produces energy for a gas or electric stove. The young Harmonists soon learn the eccentricities of a wood fire. The new residents soon discover how this one difference can tremendously influence a life style. The apprentice cabinetmakers find they are the source of power while using a plane and draw-knife to fashion their candle-holder. To their dismay, the Brothers learn that the function of the invisible sewage system they have always taken for granted was once performed by boys emptying the slop barrel. This is, by the way, the least favorite chore of the day. The amount of water used by a household is etched in their minds after carrying each bucket of water to the house and carrying the waste water away. As the experience progresses, they begin to realize that technology governs not only a physical act, but regulates one's life style and influences one's intellectual frame of reference.[4]

It is interesting to watch youngsters performing actual chores and enjoying doing so. Older people can look back and recall that it wasn't all fun to sweep floors and make beds, and yet for children brought up in an age of vacuum cleaners, electric dishwashers, garbage disposals, frozen TV dinners, actually participating in running a home for a brief period is fascinating.

And, Mrs. Reibel maintains, this program could be conducted successfully in any one-room restoration, a log cabin, for example.

---

4. Black, *The Live-In at Old Economy*, p. 7.

Choice of Personnel for School Groups

What type of person can handle school groups successfully? Mary Mason Holt, formerly in charge of school tours at the Valentine Museum in Richmond, Virginia, maintains that docents who conduct school groups have to have "a love of children and an ability to handle them under the most trying circumstances. Also a good pair of feet that will last for hours!"[5]

No one should ever be assigned to conduct a school group who does not have a genuine love for children. It takes infinite patience to answer the almost endless questions children will ask, to ignore the pushing and shoving that will sometimes occur, and to turn a deaf ear to shuffling feet and excited voices. An interpreter has to have an understanding of children's interests and must avoid imposing an adult lecture on them. He has to be willing to remove himself from center stage in order to let children participate in interpretation under skillful guidance. He has to be the type who can have fun with children, but can still exhibit enough authority to handle discipline problems. (If some occur, he would do well to take a good look at the type of interpretation he is giving. It may be boring them to death.) He must be the type who can keep his poise, even when a child is sick at his stomach in the middle of a tour. And he must know a lot of answers to a lot of unusual questions.

In addition, guides working with children must have an open attitude about questions. They should not assume the responsibility of answering all questions or even of being able to do so. Instead, they should sometimes say such things as, "How can we find an answer to that question?" Or "Is there only one *right* answer?"

Training personnel for school groups. A person conducting school tours should have the same type of training to answer questions and to interpret the exhibitions as a person regularly assigned to interpret for adult groups. In addition, those who work with children should try to inform themselves about modern educational techniques, so that they really will understand

5. Letter, Mary Mason Holt to Shirley P. Low.

how to help children learn something about their history. Many guides are going to have to be willing to *unlearn* former teaching methods and learn new methods that have been found to be more effective.

Value of school tours. Each site must decide for itself what it will do for school groups. Special programs can be very elaborate, or relatively simple, depending on the site's order of priorities and the resources upon which it can draw. For many sites, a special program is impossible; it is difficult just to keep open. But for most sites, there are substantial rewards to be received from setting up some kind of special interpretation for school groups. This helps youthful visitors to learn from the site and helps determine whether those children, as mature adults, will regard sites as places worthy of support or will dismiss them as playthings for elderly antiquarians. Whatever is attempted should be done in concert with the teachers who will be bringing groups to the site, and it should utilize the experience of other historic sites that have found successful ways of meeting their responsibilities.

If historic sites develop the right attitude toward school groups and really welcome them, instead of thinking of them as an intrusion, if they create a meaningful program on the children's level, and if they recruit well-trained personnel to work with children, they will find the results rewarding. A group of children reliving their heritage is an inspiring sight, and it is up to the interpreter to help those children see the relationship between history and themselves.

7

Selection of Interpreters

SINCE the interpreter plays such a key role in the forming of visitor judgments about the site, one might expect that the administrators of most sites would select their interpreters with great care. There are, however, few historic site jobs that are given so little thought. Many organizations are more careful about the selection of maintenance personnel than they are about interpreters. Much of the bad interpretation—or lack of interpretation—at historic sites can be blamed on the selection of interpreters for their presumed ability to launder curtains or mow grass in their spare time; or their political activities; or the misconception that the interpreter, whether professional or volunteer, need only know enough to show visitors the downstairs before the upstairs; or the willingness of the site to settle for a bargain-basement tour of its expensive restoration by persons whose main qualifications are a willingness to work for less than the minimum wage.

These kinds of hiring practices reflect a gross underestimation of the responsibilities of the interpreter and the importance of interpretation to the success of the site. The good interpreter, after all, must possess knowledge of the site, a great deal of physical stamina coupled with diplomacy, mature judgment, an ability to relate to other people, a sympathetic and patient attitude toward visitors, a firmness in controlling groups of people, and a coolness in handling emergencies. The late Christopher Rand, writing about his "Travels in Greece" in a *New Yorker* article, described the job of historic site guide as calling for "a combined teacher, nurse, mother, diplomat, and geisha girl"—a tall order, particularly for male interpreters.

An interpreter's background and education should be appropriate to the assignment. Here, a knowledge of root vegetables is called for.— *Sleepy Hollow Restorations*

What qualifications should a site administrator look for in trying to recruit such a paragon as Rand has described?

Education and experience. First, administrators should seek a person whose education and background are appropriate to the interpretive assignment at hand. A person who is expected to interpret a blacksmith's shop, for example, will need experience in blacksmithing and in working with blacksmith's tools more than he will a college degree. A guide for the home of Brigham Young, the Mormon leader, on the other hand, will need an educational background adequate to the discussion of Mormon theology and history.

Since the traveling public is mostly from the middle and upper income groups, in which college education is increasingly common, it will be helpful if guides have some college experience. The study of substantive subjects, whether within or outside the academic curriculum, usually indicates a capacity for the further study that should be a part of the training and development of a good interpreter. But many good guides have no education beyond high school. Regardless of formal education, a person who has read and studied widely and who knows how to meet the public graciously is usually a good prospect.

A cultivated background is desirable, but it is important that the prospective interpreter does not assume that he has all the answers and therefore does not need further study. The best potential interpreters approach the job with a good deal of humility and with a recognition that a vast amount of specialized knowledge will be needed if one is to interpret the site in a significant manner and answer correctly the questions visitors may ask about historic events and personalities, architecture and gardens, the decorative arts, and many other subjects. Furthermore, an interpreter should expect to continue acquiring helpful information. Continuing research and reading will often turn up facts that throw a different light on traditional stories long associated with the site. A good interpreter will grow on the job and will not be afraid to let cherished legends die if they are proved doubtful.

An interpreter's speech should be free of grammatical errors and without an accent so strong that the interpretation will be difficult to understand for visitors from other areas of the country. He should speak clearly and distinctly in a voice that is easily heard by all but, at the same time, without shrillness or an unpleasant raucous quality.

Personality. It is very important that the interpreter have a pleasing personality. Visitors should not be greeted by a cold, unfriendly, disgruntled, impatient, uninterested guide. Nothing helps them forget aching feet and weary miles of driving faster than an interpreter who greets them with a friendly smile and a warm, genuine interest in their well-being. In interviewing the ·prospective interpreters, therefore, administrators should look for evidence of a genuine liking for all kinds of people—the people who are attractive, well-dressed, well-behaved, and well-informed, and also those who are sloppy, fussy, ignorant, and uncooperative. One should also look for indications of patience, graciousness, and compassion that will persist, no matter how trying the circumstances. Long after a visitor has returned home, he may look back on his visit to a historic site with real affection, not because he recalls all the historic facts about it, but because he remembers the warmth and friendliness of the person who interpreted the site to him.

And *effective* interpreters must have enthusiasm. They must project a conviction that what they are doing is important and exciting. Enthusiasm for what might otherwise seem dull, dry historic facts, can make them memorable. The attitude of guides toward their job and toward the story they have to tell is catching—for better or worse.

Physical qualifications. Interpreters need stamina and lots of it. They must be in good physical condition to take the standing, walking, and talking that are involved in presenting the historic site. They are bound to get tired, of course, but no matter how the feet ache, how weary the voice from talking all day, how "people-tired" they are from hordes of visitors, good interpreters must somehow keep from letting the weariness show. The last tour of the day should be given with the same

A friendly smile and genuine interest help the most in creating effective interpretation and good visitor response.—*Fort Point, National Park Service*

exuberance as the first, *because the last tour group is as important as the first.*

As to appearance, good interpreters will not dress for work as if they were going to a party or to a picnic at the beach. The kind of clothing worn to an office or to teach school is usually appropriate. The main thing is a clean, neat appearance at all times.

It should not be necessary to stress the need for cleanliness and personal hygiene, but experience with guides in many parts of the country indicates that some need to be reminded. Historic sites often have small rooms, poor ventilation, and crowded conditions which can contribute to an unpleasant experience if care is not taken to avoid offensive odors and overwhelming perfumes.

Physical stamina and the ability to shine despite aching feet are part of an interpreter's professional requirements.—*Old Economy Village; photograph by Charles Parkhurst*

Professional attitude. One of the attributes most to be desired in a guide is a professional attitude. This is difficult to define, but among other things it means doing what one is supposed to do without constant supervision. It also means going beyond the bare requirements of the job, when necessary, without thought of reward. People with professional attitudes have enough respect for the job and for themselves to do what needs to be done to the best of their ability, never letting the museum or themselves down. A professional attitude also means that the guide will not discuss the museum's policies on working conditions, pay, or anything else of that type before guests; nor talk about his personal life and problems in front of guests; nor risk offending guests by expressing personal opinions on contemporary controversial issues.

Volunteers. Everything that has been said thus far about what makes a good interpreter applies to volunteers, as well as to those who work for pay. Most historic sites would have to close their doors if it were not for the dedicated volunteers who give generously of their time and talents. These volunteers come from a number of sources; some of the best are from service organizations, notable among which has been the Junior League. Many volunteers are people with regular jobs whose enthusiasm for a site induces them to work as guides on their days off. Many retired people find the interpretation of historic sites a rewarding use of talents and skills developed over a lifetime of work and study. Finally, many volunteers are young housewives whose parental responsibilities preclude their accepting regular employment but who have ability and vitality to bring to the interpreter's job.

Unfortunately, volunteer interpreters have acquired a reputation for being undependable. In many ways this is a consequence of the failure of the historic site organization to make interpretation the challenge it ought to be for a talented volunteer. Too often, the position of volunteer guide is offered as: "You don't have to know anything. Just read the brochure and you'll do fine. The main thing is just to have somebody on duty." When management regards interpretation as so unskilled and unimportant, volunteers are not likely to take seriously the need for them to show up for duty.

Almost without exception, sites that have truly effective volunteer guide programs have made them important. They have insisted that everybody cannot be an interpreter, that being an interpreter requires both talent and training. Then they have not only provided opportunities for training—lectures, printed materials, group tours to other sites—but made beginner's training and continuing training mandatory for persons who wish to remain on the interpreter roster. They have also worked to make the volunteer guide program fun for its participants, with occasional parties, guest lectures, and other special events just for the interpreters—volunteer and paid alike. Under these circumstances, interpreters feel fortunate to have been selected, grateful for what they have learned in their training, gratified to be doing something really important, and just a little apprehensive that, if they do not appear when they are scheduled, someone else will be given their place. Obtaining these results is not easy; but it can be done if the historic site organization begins by recognizing that interpreting is a professional job which only volunteers who can give a professional performance should be privileged to hold, and if it also provides its volunteers with the kind of job satisfaction that will compensate for the absence of salary.

Recruiting Interpreters

Where is the best place for the historic site organization to look for its professional guides? There are a number of potentially good sources in almost any community: retired school teachers or military officers; young people just out of college who have not quite settled on their future careers; women whose children are old enough that they are not demanding of their mothers' time; women whose other home responsibilities have diminished or widows who suddenly find their lives empty and who are in need of an outlet for special talents that may have lain dormant while they were absorbed in the routine of rearing a family. It is important to note that many colleges and universities are beginning to train students in historical society and museum work. These students need summer employment for experience in their chosen field and after graduation are prime prospects for staff positions.

If the site has a mixture of paid and volunteer interpreters, its first step in hiring a new, paid interpreter should be to review the volunteer staff for an able person who has reached the state of wanting permanent employment. Word-of-mouth announcements of job openings frequently bring in applicants who are congenial with the present staff. And do not overlook the possibilities of newspaper advertisements.

Pay and benefits. In the past, wages paid to interpreters in historic sites have been notoriously low. The reasons are that historic site organizations have been accustomed to regard interpreters as unskilled people, rather than professionals, and because the organizations have long existed in a state of genteel poverty. Low wages have only occasionally attracted really competent interpreters, and the level of performance of most interpreters has not justified higher wages.

With the rapid increase of professionalism in historical organizations, the persistence of low wages is breaking down. At the same time, an increasingly sophisticated visiting public has come more and more to expect good interpretation. Sites that aspire to keep up with the times and come up to the expectations of their visitors must therefore adopt a realistic policy of compensation for the interpretive staff.

It is not easy to establish standards of pay. The financial resources, amount of visitation, hours, and other variables of each site have to be taken into consideration. Sites with heavy visitation and substantial budgets may find it reasonable to peg the salaries of interpreters at the prevailing salaries for public school teachers with comparable education and experience. After all, the guide's job of interpreting the past is, or should be, just as important as teaching in the classroom. Smaller sites, on the other hand, may not be able to equal teacher salaries because they frequently pay their directors at that rate; but they cannot pay appreciably less and expect to attract good guide applicants. A salary that is too low, after all,

A guide's job—interpreting the past—should be as important as teaching in the classroom.—*State Historical Society of Wisconsin*

demeans both the site and the interpreter, to the disadvantage of both.

In addition to salary, some consideration should be given to fringe benefits of employment. If the professional interpreter is to work weekends, he should be off duty on regularly designated weekdays. He should also receive an annual vacation with pay, usually not less than two weeks, after the completion of one full year's employment. The site organization should also provide the interpreter with compensatory time off whenever he works—as frequently is the case—on holidays and on regular days off when visitation is especially heavy.

Perhaps the most important additional benefit is hospital-surgical insurance. It is becoming standard practice to provide such insurance, and it is important protection for the employee. Some organizations pay the entire cost of the insurance; others share the cost with the employee. If the staff of the historic site is not big enough to qualify for a group policy, the site may contribute to the premiums paid by staff members on individually owned policies. If those payments are made directly to the insurance company, they afford the same tax treatment for the employee as a museum-furnished group health policy.

The best-financed sites may want to offer their staff members a retirement plan. This can be a very important fringe benefit in attracting and holding well-qualified interpreter applicants. In this connection, the site administrator should be aware that recent federal legislation makes it illegal to force employees to retire before age 70, and that some states make it illegal to force retirement at any age.

The key to developing a good interpretive staff is attracting good people to do the job. The age-old incentives to accomplish this are giving the interpreter a sense of important accomplishment and some kind of reward for good effort, whether in money, prestige, or other personal benefits. Interpretation has all the necessary excitement and challenge to attract good people. What has been lacking at a great many sites is recognition of the crucial importance of interpretation to the site's success and a consequent failure to provide the kind of incentives that will get good people who, with proper training, can become good guides.

8

Training of Interpreters

IF a historic site organization wants quality interpretation, it must be willing to spend time and money on the training of beginning personnel and on the continued training of interpreters as long as they work at the site. There are many complaints about poor interpretation at historic sites, but who is really to blame? A good site organization will take steps to recruit high-caliber personnel to begin with, then see that they are properly prepared for their jobs, and finally give major attention to their continued competence in their jobs, whether those interpreters are volunteers or paid staff.

Even if the site should be fortunate enough to employ people who meet the highest standards for potential interpreters, newcomers will need to learn all of the unique details and techniques that contribute to an accurate, intelligent interpretation of the site. They will also have to learn how to control tour traffic and maintain security. Interpreters need specialized training before they start to work, so that they will be properly prepared to handle the job. They also need a continuing education program that will enable them to grow on the job. *Training* applies to such specifics as the facts an interpreter will cover in particular places, the procedures that should be followed in moving through the site, the rules concerning interpretation procedures, and the handling of emergencies. *Education*, on the other hand, applies to the guides' acquiring not only basic facts but, through continuing study, a depth of understanding of the site and its history that will enable them to enrich their interpretation for visitors.

Some beginners resent having to study before they start to work as interpreters. They want the glamour without the hard work attached. Others feel that, because they were born and reared in an atmosphere of historic lore, they have no need for further study. Good interpreters, on the other hand, welcome all the information they can get. They feel more secure in their jobs if they are confident they have received accurate information and know how to present it to guests.

Purposes of Training

The main purposes in the training of interpreters for historic sites are these:

1. To give personnel basic, comprehensive information about the historic site, and to place it in the context of other sites in the area. Such data should include details of historic events, historic personages, ways of life of the time, architectural details, furnishings and their use, and the physical features of the outdoor settings. It should also include information on such mundane, nonhistorical matters as the nearest garage for car repairs, locations of nearby restaurants, and other facts about which questions can be anticipated.

2. To teach both new and experienced staff members what they should know to interpret the various types of historic sites. Various categories of information would include these:

Documentary. Historic events and personages involved; the type of life characteristic of the times; architecture of the buildings; the site's furnishings and their use; the gardens—their style and plant materials; restoration of the site—the evidence and the people responsible.

Representative. Family life represented; social life; education; religion; ways of making a living; crafts; professions; types of homes; type and use of furnishings; styles of gardens and plant life; the restoration of the site; the evidence and the people responsible.

Aesthetic. Details of architecture, furniture, and gardens; the restoration of the site, the evidence and the people responsible.

3. To teach techniques of handling groups—getting organized; moving as a group through the building; keeping control; avoiding accidents; taking care of emergencies; protecting the collections; promoting good public relations.

4. To teach operation of audio-visual equipment and repair of temporary breakdowns of equipment.

5. To coach interpreters in speaking well and developing effective voice control.

Types of Training

The amount and kind of training that interpreters receive vary greatly from site to site according to the financial abilities and priorities of various site organizations. Only a few organizations can invest the kind of time and money that has gone into the highly structured formal training programs at the larger, more affluent sites, but every site can do more than it is doing at present to provide its visitors with the best possible tour experience.

The simplest form of preparing newcomers to be interpreters is to assign them for a few days to observe good, experienced interpreters on real tours. The beginner thus has a chance to see a successful guide not only give the interpretation, but control traffic, maintain security, and answer questions. This is a useful component of an over-all training program, but by itself it has a number of limitations. Obviously, one cannot learn all that should be known about the site, its history, the people who lived there, the furnishings, and the restoration in just a few days. Word-of-mouth training also allows errors to creep into the interpretation, as successive "generations" of beginners become trainers for newer beginners. Finally, in a few days of this kind of training, one confronts only a small percentage of the problems that will have to be solved by the interpreter after the training period is over.

A very important component of many training programs is the periodic meeting of the interpretation staff, both volunteers and professionals, to discuss frequently encountered problems. An example of the content of an informal discussion session on problems interpreters have encountered at Stratford Hall, the birthplace of Robert E. Lee, illustrates the kinds of topics that smaller sites might need to discuss:

Questions for April 2 Discussion

Please be prepared to discuss how you would answer the following questions asked by visitors at Stratford Hall recently:

Procedures
1. How do we get to the Mill?
2. Are you guides allowed to accept tips?
3. My grandfather will be here in a minute—he's in a wheelchair and will be a little slow. May we join your group?
4. But the barrier was open a little and I wanted to get a closer look at this pistol!
5. I think this place is a gyp! The five of us paid $6.25 to get in here, and we certainly haven't seen very much for all that money. And now you say everything is closing.

The Appearance of Stratford Hall
1. How much reconstruction has been done on the house?
2. The last time I was here, the outside woodwork was painted brownish-red. What happened?
3. The river must have been closer in colonial days.
4. What kind of grass do you plant? The lawns are so green for this time of year.
5. Does the Garden Club do your flower arrangements?

Furnishings
1. You said that picture is of "punch-work" and silk embroidery. What is the difference between "punch-work" and "stump-work"?
2. Did they use tablecloths? We haven't seen any on dining tables in these houses.

The Lee Family
1. Now, tell me if this is true: I have always heard that Robert E. Lee's mother was buried alive and that a slave heard her screaming down in the vault and let her out. This

took place three years before Robert was born and there are medical records in Washington, D. C., to prove it. Do you know anything about this? [This is a good example of legends that get started and which have to be discounted politely.]

2. Which of the family was a medical doctor at one time?

Miscellaneous

1. We didn't hear what you said about this room. Would you mind saying it over again?

2. Do you know the name of the director from Missouri?

3. I thought I read on a plaque at the gatehouse that this place was owned by the National Park Service.

4. What does the "grist" in "gristmill" mean?

These problem-solving sessions can be very useful, but one must plan them carefully to void getting bogged down in the minutiae of techniques without extending the abilities and understanding of the interpreters.

Many sites have found it useful to supplement these kinds of training sessions with more substantive lectures on the history of the period to which the site belongs. Some sites have regular programs featuring speakers on political, economic, and social history; the decorative arts; architecture; antiques; and other topics. These lectures, planned specifically for the paid and volunteer interpreters, not only broaden the knowledge of the guides, but provide attractive side benefits for the job of interpreter. They are an extra inducement for volunteer guides to stay in good standing so that they may participate.

One means of achieving greater uniformity of interpretation is to reduce to writing the techniques of a good interpreter. The following excerpt from the interpretation of the Feast Hall at Old Economy is taken from *A Manual for Guides, Docents, Hostesses, and Volunteers of Old Economy*, by Daniel B. Reibel and Patricia Black Reibel (Ambridge, Pennsylvania: The Harmonie Associates, Inc., 1974), and is used with permission.

The Feast Hall

Point to stress: The Feast Hall was the center of the cultural life of the

Harmony Society. Its major purpose was to furnish a place for one of the Society's major religious events.

Interpretation: The visitor enters the Village through the Feast Hall, where he is greeted by the person on duty as receptionist. He is then invited to view the exhibit rooms while waiting for the tour to begin. If a tour is just beginning, he is told he may return to the Feast Hall at the conclusion of his tour. As a guide, your first introduction to the visitor is to ask him to come to the schoolroom for the presentation of orientation film, 'Those Who Believed.' You should introduce yourself to your group. You will be able to establish a rapport with them much more quickly by identifying yourself at the beginning of your tour.

Dialogue: "Welcome to Old Economy, the third and final home of the Harmony Society. I am _____, your guide for your tour of the village. Before we begin the tour, I would like to show you Old Economy's orientation film, Those Who Believed' " [The film lasts 18 minutes, during which time the guide should sit on a bench in the hall . . . to greet late-comers to the group.]

. . .

Feast Hall (Saal)

Method: Particularly with large tours, it is advisable for the tour to be seated in this room. The adult schoolroom and the Feast Hall provide the only real opportunities to talk to a large group as a cohesive unit—so it is best to take advantage of it.

Dialogue: "George Rapp and his followers emigrated to the United States from their native Germany in order to practice their religious beliefs as they saw them. Father Rapp, as he came to be called, had a religious experience that compelled him to begin gathering people around him to discuss the relationship of the individual with God. Perhaps they did not realize it, but they were part of a much larger religious movement, pietism, which was sweeping both Europe and the United States. Essentially, the pietists felt that each man must have a direct and individual relationship with God. They believed in the priesthood of every man. Because of their feelings of brotherhood, the pietists in general were pacifists. In practice, they were skeptical of organized churches because they felt that the structure of priests and ministers hindered rather than helped man in his search for salvation. In the United States, some members of this loosely defined movement came to be known as the come-outers because they 'came out' of their organized churches in order to form organizations of their own.

. . .

"The use of the Feast Hall shows how the activities of the community were a combination of both the religious and the secular. In a religious community it is virtually impossible to separate the two areas of life. The Society held the *liebesmahl* or love feast in this room. While the love feast may not have been a true sacrament, it certainly had many of the aspects of a sacrament of the church. When the Society gathered for the feast, the men sat on one side of the room and the women on the other, with the trustees at a long table in the front of the room. The feast combined a meal, sermon, and music with the Society all participating in the spirit of the brotherhood. The feasts were held at various times during the year, such as at Christmas; in February to celebrate the founding of the Society; at Easter; and for the Harvest festival. They may have had as many as eight or more in some years, because they seemed to tell each traveler who wrote about them a different number."

. . .

Items of Interest:

1. Printing press. This machine may have been built in 1822, but the first use was late in 1824. The press was actually first used in Harmony, Indiana after the time the Society was in the process of moving to Pennsylvania. It was operated by the doctor (J. C. Müller), who learned printing from an itinerant printer. The press is a typical wood press, which today is called "Franklin hand press." It may have been built by the Harmony Society. The other equipment belongs to the press.

2. Static Electricity machine. This machine, with its large glass wheel, was used in experiments. It was used in the adult school and was probably purchased before 1830.

3. Book cupboards. These two large cupboards sit in the adult schoolroom. They were used to hold the library. From details of construction and hardware, they appear to be rather late, say, after 1860.[1]

A Suggested Interpreter Study Program

The following training program incorporates elements of a number of the more successful interpretive programs around the country. It can be modified to suit the individual requirements of different sites. The techniques it recommends are within the capabilities of most sites.

Questions and references. Provide each trainee with a list of questions or a syllabus containing the basic information that is

1. Reibel, *Manual for Guides*, 14-19.

needed to interpret a site accurately and to answer anticipated questions, together with references to recommended reading. The questions for discussion should be simple and to the point, with answers easily available in the books or notes provided. Actual page references for each question are helpful.

Discuss the questions with each individual trainee so that he knows whether he has obtained accurate information. During the discussion periods, the trainee should be told where he is likely to use this particular information, either in interpreting a particular room or in answering commonly asked questions.

Discussions should be as informal as possible. Many historic site interpreters are retired people or others who have not studied recently. They are likely to be intimidated by a too-formidable list of references and by too-formal discussions of the reading.

If for some reason a trainee has not been able to find answers to the questions, the person in charge of interpretation should not hesitate to give him the answers. There should be no idea of trying to "catch" a trainee unprepared. The emphasis should be on helping him to know the details necessary for good interpretation. In some cases, the immediate need for certain kinds of information may not be apparent, but the trainee should be assured that all the information he is acquiring will eventually fall into place and that he will feel more secure in answering questions because of his growing store of factual details.

Visual aids such as maps, pictures, filmstrips, slides, and movies may be used to supplement the instructional sessions.

Lectures by experts in history, the decorative arts, architecture, gardens, and related topics are helpful for all the interpreters, but for beginners, formal lectures should be thought of as supplementary to informal discussions on ways to present the historic site accurately and effectively. Formal lectures are not as worthwhile as informal discussions in setting a pattern for effective presentation of the site to visitors.

Tours of site. The new trainee should be taken on a tour of the entire historic site by an experienced, and effective interpreter, in order to become familiar with the architecture, the furnishings, the gardens, and other physical features, as well as the interpretive facilities. The tour should demonstrate ways for beginners to use the information they have been learning. It should also emphasize the techniques of handling groups and providing effective security for the collections.

Demonstration tours. The person doing the training should demonstrate with real visitors how to interpret the historic site. This will help trainees to know what to say in order to accomplish the objectives, what questions are likely to be asked, and how to manage a group. This is one of the most helpful procedures in training a new person.

New interpreters should not be told to listen to just anyone's interpretation. Some interpreters understandably are better than others—more interesting to hear, more accurate, better able to handle groups of people, more conscious of what is important and what is not, and better able to impart information systematically in order to accomplish the major objectives which the historic site hopes to stress for visitors.

Beginners should be urged not to incorporate into their own interpretation information that they have acquired through listening to other interpreters or have picked up from visitors. Legends abound in any historic site, and simple facts get twisted into fantastic tales. Every effort should be made to prevent the spread of stories that cannot be authenticated by reference to reliable books, research reports, or information given by the person doing the training during discussion sessions or demonstrations.

The person in charge of interpretation, or an equally well-qualified and experienced person, should do the demonstration tours. He should show the new interpreters how to adapt basic interpretations to the interests of the group and how to stay within the time available for the tour; how to answer questions accurately and avoid being monopolized by one or two guests; how to control a group so that it moves when it is necessary to move but without giving people the impression that they are being hurried through an exhibition; how to avoid accidents and to guarantee as far as possible the protection of furnishings.

At the same time, the person doing the demonstration tour should discourage trainees from imitating exactly what he has said in his interpretation; or if standard sample interpretations are available, from memorizing what has been printed. The demonstration interpretation and the printed "scripts" should be thought of as guides only. Each interpreter should be urged to develop his own particular way of presenting a historic site to the public, centered around the objectives of the site.

Clearing interpretations. Prospective interpreters should discuss what they are going to say with the person in charge of interpretation. In this way, errors can be eliminated before they are perpetuated. Also, each person can be checked to determine whether he is placing emphasis where the organization wants it.

In these clearing sessions, individuals should not be encouraged to repeat, word for word, what they expect to say to guests, for fear they will be tempted to memorize their interpretations. Rather, they should be asked to cover the major points they plan to make in each area throughout the historic site. They should also be asked to show that they understand the procedures for reporting for work, gathering groups, and conducting visitors through the site; and they should be spot-checked on furnishings, architectural details, plantings, and the like.

Trainees may dread this oral test. At this point, they will sense that they must know a great deal if they are to interpret a historic site well, that the grace period of preparation is about over, and that they will soon be plunged into the reality of facing the visiting public. People who have not studied or worked for a long time will be more apprehensive than recent students or former teachers. For this reason, clearing sessions should begin with casual conversations before plunging into the serious business of determining whether the trainee knows how to interpret a historic site successfully.

Oral examinations are preferable to written ones for a number of reasons. In the first place, the oral examination is really another teaching session in which the material to be covered is reviewed and its use indicated. Also, if there are several trainees, they will learn from each other under this kind of guidance. Furthermore, the informal discussion reveals how well a person expresses himself orally in the way he will have to do when he interprets a historic site. Finally, a written examination might terrify those who have not recently studied formally.

If the person conducting the clearing sessions feels that a trainee has not learned the necessary facts, or does not understand how to organize and present the material in an orderly and significant way, he should ask the trainee to study further. Sometimes it is obvious that a particular trainee will never make the grade. If this happens with an applicant for a paid job, he should be asked to consider some other work better suited to his talents. If the trainee is a volunteer, the solution should be the same. Great tact will be required, of course, but the site should not use a poor interpreter because he or she will work without pay.

Throughout the training sessions for new people, the person doing the training should impress upon trainees that interpreting a historic site is an important and responsible undertaking. Interpreters should respect the importance of the historic site and have sufficient pride in themselves and their own performance not to consider attempting to interpret it without being certain they can do a good job.

Checking performance on the job. After interpreters have worked long enough to feel somewhat secure, their performance on the job should be evaluated. This can be done in a number of ways. Some historic sites have the person who trained the interpreters visit them on the job. This should be done as inconspicuously as possible, so that visitors will not be aware that the interpreter is being observed. The person being observed, however, should be aware of it. It is not good for the morale of interpreters to be spied on behind their backs.

The person doing the observing should check on the quality of interpretation; the interpreter's ability to handle groups; personal characteristics, such as voice, mannerisms, poise, appearance; public relations; attitude; and evidence of progress; and should make recommendations for improvement. At the larger sites, this observation of interpreters is part of the periodic review of salaries and possible promotions. Following the observation, the person who has done the observing should hold a conference with the interpreter involved and keep a confidential record of the observation.

Though interpreters may dread this type of observation, after it is over they are usually glad that they have been evaluated. If they are doing well, they are pleased to be reassured. If they need improvement, they usually sense this themselves and are grateful for help and encouragement.

Some historic sites have found it useful to ask interpreters to evaluate their own interpretations. By making use of a self-audit sheet such as the following, the interpreter is reminded of the standards of his job and is assisted in identifying areas in which he needs help.

SELF-EVALUATION QUESTIONNAIRE

Interpretation of Facts

_____ Was I able to bring this historic event or personage alive for my guests? If not, why not? _____

_____ Did I select appropriate details to accomplish the objectives of this historic site? What else might I have included? _____

_____ Did I organize what I said so that visitors could understand the major points I was making?

_____ Could I answer all the questions asked about historic events and personages? _____ About architecture and furnishings? _____ About the grounds?

_____ Did I hold the interest of my group?

Procedures

_____ Did I keep my group under control?

_____ Did I observe recommended procedures for the orderly showing of this historic site?

Personal Relations

_____ Was I gracious and helpful to visitors? If not, what do I need to do to improve? _____

_____ Was I cooperative with my fellow workers, and did I carry my full share of responsibility? If not, what do I need to do to improve? _____

Personal Characteristics

____ Is my speech pleasant to listen to and effective? If not, what do I need to do to improve? _____

____ Am I appropriately groomed for working as an interpreter of a historic site?

____ Am I performing my job conscientiously and in a professional manner?

Some historic sites have made use of video or audio recorders. Interpreters who can see and hear themselves delivering their presentations, may discover that they have fallen into rote patterns that should be corrected. The self-evaluation questions given above could be used in this type of evaluation also. If individuals are very self-conscious about being recorded on tape, this type of evaluation will not be effective.

In most situations, it is not a good idea for the director of a historic site to ask one interpreter to evaluate the presentation of another interpreter. Many people resent evaluation by their peers. It can lead to very poor morale among the interpretive staff.

Continuing Education

No matter how many years a person has worked for a historic site, he cannot possibly know all there is to be known about its historic events and personages, the way of life it represents, its decorative arts, architecture, gardens, and everything else associated with it. Research should be continued, so that new information will contribute to new understandings of the site and its history.

Purposes for continuing education. The main purposes of continuing training of experienced interpreters are much the same as those for beginning training:

1. To gain information in the same categories as those covered in beginning training, but in greater depth, in order to enrich the basic interpretation of the historic site.

2. To add to the backlog of information an interpreter needs to answer visitors' questions.

3. To improve techniques in handling visitors and in public relations.

Continuing training may also be useful for the additional purposes of preparing selected individuals for special assignments, such as talks to special-interest groups or escorting VIP's and foreign visitors; helping interpreters develop and maintain fresh approaches to their work; and providing remedial training for those who need it—principally in speech, organization, and mannerisms. Again, comprehensive study gives an interpreter security in answering questions and flexibility in interpretation.

If a staff of interpreters is small, formal continuing training may be impractical. Essential topics, however, can be covered informally. The person responsible for interpretation can provide a syllabus and a bibliography for supervised reading. The results of such informal training can be evaluated in conversations and in direct observation on duty. If there is a college nearby, a staff can be encouraged to take classes there or to take correspondence courses from other colleges on topics related to the interpretation of the site.

Small historic sites in a given area can profitably combine their efforts, not only to produce necessary research, but to train their interpreters well. Several years ago, for example, historic sites in the vicinity of Nashville, Tennessee, including Traveller's Rest, Oaklands, Cragfont, Belle Meade, and the Tennessee Botanical Gardens and Fine Arts Center, pooled their resources to sponsor a series of lectures by nationally recognized authorities on architecture and the decorative arts, and by experts on the history of Nashville and Tennessee. Visiting authorities supplemented their talks with individual site consultations at no additional travel costs! The lecture series gave interpreters from all the sites a broader perspective on the place of their site in the historical and cultural growth of the area, while the consultations provided specific help on individual interpretations. An additional bonus was an important fringe benefit provided for volunteers who gave so freely of their time as interpreters of the cooperating sites.

If a historic site has a large staff, however, continuing training can be developed in a more formal manner. For example:

1. Specialists on topics of general interest can give lectures to the entire group on such topics as: "Future Plans for This Historic Site," "Other Restorations of Interest in This Community (State, Nation) and their Relationship to Each Other," "Recent Excavations at ___ Site," "New Developments in the Historic Preservation Program."

2. Regular courses at graduate level can be offered, in history, geography, government, social life, the decorative arts, architecture, gardens, costumes of the period, public relations, administrative problems, principles of interpretation, and other pertinent subjects. Usually, all personnel should attend classes in each category. A syllabus and a bibliography should be provided for each course.

3. Specialized training can be provided for those qualified to do garden or antiques tours, or to participate in other special programs, such as the opening of private houses for special tours.

These courses can be taught by qualified staff personnel, local teachers or college professors, retired experts, or other specialists.

Training seminars and workshops. Historic site organizations should also take advantage of the increasing number of seminars and workshops that are held throughout the country under the sponsorship of national organizations and state historical agencies. The American Association for State and Local History continues to conduct general seminars on the interpretation of history by historical museums and sites, and has produced an independent study kit on *Basic Historic Site Interpretation* for use by groups and individuals. Regional and state museum associations also run occasional, specialized seminars on historic sites and interpretation.

Both AASLH and the American Association of Museums have published material that can be very useful to interpreters. Their magazines, *History News* and *Museum News*, publish many articles on successful—and sometimes unsuccessful—interpretation programs. The Technical Leaflet series of AASLH and a number of books from the AASLH Press shed further light on historic sites and their presentation to the public. Membership in one or both of these organizations can be very helpful in providing information about training programs and the latest developments in the field.

Tours of other historic sites. If a historic site can afford it, it should arrange for its interpreters to tour other historic sites occasionally. If the budget will not allow such expenditures as travel expenses, meals, and, in some cases, overnight accommodations for interpreters, at least the site should make it possible for them to have time off at their own expense for such trips.

These tours are valuable for a number of reasons. Interpreters will find it helpful to learn more about other historic sites in the area so that they can round out their own knowledge and answer questions of visitors. Also, it is valuable for interpreters of different historic sites to get together and compare notes on their experiences. And it is always rewarding to observe how others interpret, both to learn what to do and what not to do.

Training records. A large historic site will probably have enough variety in all its training courses to make it worthwhile to keep records of each individual's training. This is an aid in assigning individuals to areas of the historic site for which they are best qualified and it is helpful in checking to see that all personnel have the necessary courses and that they progress from year to year through other enriching courses. The record form should contain such data about the interpreter as name, address, telephone number, and date employed. In addition, the record should indicate when the interpreter began and ended each training program and what the employee is qualified to interpret: a historic house, a battlefield, a furniture museum, gardens, etc. If advanced training is given, a record should be made of the courses the interpreter has had in such subjects as history, government, the decorative arts, architecture, archaeology, gardens, costumes, interpretation, and public relations. If trips to other historic sites have been available, these, too, should be noted.

Through this type of record-keeping, the administration can

know who among their staff of interpreters is particularly well-qualified for specific assignments.

The *"finished" product*. The training of interpreters at a historic site is never done. The more one learns, the more one realizes there is to be learned. Each innovation should inspire a desire to find other new and enriching ways of interpreting the site. The work as a result should never be dull.

Extensive training is expensive, but it pays off. Interpreters will grow in self-confidence and in the ability to interpret the historic site; and the site itself will enhance its reputation by having a corps of carefully selected, well-trained interpreters who are not only effective in conveying to visitors an understanding of the significance of the site, but who add measurably to the visitors' enjoyment of the site.

Extensive training pays off in self-confident, skilled interpreters who can add to the visitor's education and enjoyment.—*Mystic Seaport; photograph by Mary Anne Stets*

9

The Interpreter and Security

P UBLIC enjoyment of a historic site depends in important ways on how smoothly the site is managed. That, in turn, depends on the organization's careful establishment of rules and procedures that will enable visitors to view the historic site comfortably and yet protect the collection and provide for the safety of both staff and visitors. At most sites, it is the interpreter's responsibility to enforce those regulations.

Security at Mount Vernon includes rope barriers that allow visitors to see entire rooms without danger to furniture or furnishings.—*The Mount Vernon Ladies' Association*

Rules and procedures that are worked out ahead of time and are fully understood by both interpreters and visitors will minimize confusion. Interpreters will feel more secure in what they are doing when procedures are standardized and rules are clearly spelled out. If each one knows specifically when he is to report for duty and who does what and when and where on the job, interpreters are less likely to bicker over their responsibilities. This will avert the possibility of having visitors to a historic site overhear such comments as "You take them, I took the last ones," or "See if she's ready," or "Now, who is supposed to be upstairs?" or "Send them on upstairs. I don't mind taking some more." If this is unnerving to the interpreters, what must it be to the visitors! At the very least, the visitor becomes bewildered, feels less than welcome, and wonders whether he is some sort of commodity instead of a welcomed guest.

It is much easier for new interpreters at a historic house to do their jobs well if the procedures and rules that they are expected to enforce are spelled out for them. New interpreters are frequently confused by contradiction in procedures and in enforcement of rules when these are left to the whims of the person in charge. Visitors are also more at ease and less resentful of rules if they are told ahead of time what is going to happen to them and what is expected of them. No one enjoys the embarrassment of unwittingly breaking rules.

A wise administration will involve the interpretive staff in the development of procedures and rules, reserving to itself the final decision. The guides' experience can be invaluable in such matters as handling groups, observing what pleases or annoys visitors, working out effective places to stand in order to be heard by the entire group and to keep groups under surveillance for security purposes, and in similar on-the-job observations.

Rules for visitors. Each historic site will have its own set of rules that apply to the special conditions of that site. Where the entire exhibit is behind barriers of one sort or another and is inaccessible to visitors, and where people move about at their own pace without a conducted tour, the rules are bound to be very simple. Usually, they are confined to notices about smoking, eating, or drinking on the premises. Where guests are conducted through furnished rooms where objects are more accessible, however, the rules need to be more detailed and precise.

Some museums use signs to tell people what they cannot do. The "Do Not Touch," "No Pets Allowed," "Keep Off the Rug" signs are familiar, and they serve a purpose. But they unquestionably detract from the realistic appearance of the exhibit and frequently their wording is ungracious. If they must be used, they should be neatly and attractively printed on suitable card stock, and they should be replaced *before* they become yellowed and fly-specked.

Some historic sites issue visitors a printed list of rules at the time the ticket is purchased. This is helpful, if the visitor can be persuaded to read it. At least it provides a backup for the interpreter who needs help enforcing rules. These written rules should always have a positive approach; they should emphasize what the visitor can do before mentioning the restrictions. A printed form containing the following might be handed to visitors at the beginning of the tour:

REGULATIONS FOR VISITING THIS HISTORIC SITE

(Name of site) wants you to enjoy your visit as much as possible. To that end, we think you will appreciate knowing the regulations that apply to all visitors.

Stay with Groups

In the house, tours are conducted by guides, and visitors must stay with their group. Guests may visit the outbuildings without group restrictions.

Photography

Guests are permitted to take pictures anywhere on the site with these restrictions:

1. Flash pictures may be taken, but the flashbulb must be covered by a shield unless it is of the electronic type.
2. Tripods may not be used in the house.
3. Equipment may not be plugged into electrical outlets.
4. Photographers must stay with the conducted tour in the house.

Sitting in the House and Outbuildings

Because most of the chairs and settees in the house are very old and fragile, however, guests are requested not to sit anywhere except in the reception area.

Handling Furnishings, Wall Coverings, and Fabrics

This historic site has a number of very fine antiques that are an irreplaceable part of our heritage. Guests are therefore requested not to touch or handle the furnishings, wall hangings, or fabrics.

Smoking, Eating, and Drinking

Again, to preserve the buildings and their antique furnishings, guests are not permitted to smoke, eat, or drink in the house or outbuildings.

Pets

Pets are not allowed in the house or outbuildings. Seeing-eye dogs, however, may accompany their owners.

Bare Feet

Because the floors in these buildings are very old, there is a danger from splinters. Visitors are required to wear shoes in all buildings and on the grounds.

Children

Children are welcome at (name of site). Very small children sometimes becomes restless, however, and may interfere with the interpretation. Out of consideration for other guests, parents with crying babies or with children who are noisy or out of control will be asked to take turns visiting a building, with one parent keeping the child outside. If parents are unwilling to do this, they may return to the desk for a refund on their tickets.

Parents must keep their children with them at all times.

Parents with babies in back carriers should watch to see that the babies do not get close enough to the furnishings to damage them.

. . .

We hope that you will find that knowing these regulations before your visit to the historic area will be of help. Have a pleasant visit.

No matter how gracefully worded such a notice may be, a long list of printed rules detracts from the warm welcome we want the visitor to feel. Before printing or posting rules, therefore, we should consider carefully which of the rules might be presented by the interpreter during the tour itself. The rules concerning smoking, eating, photography, disruptive children, and bare feet will probably need to be posted or distributed where the tickets are sold. They are conditions applying to the privilege of taking the tour. Since they also govern activities in which visitors may already be engaged when they first meet their interpreter, there is no way the rules can then be announced without embarrassing a guest who had no way of knowing he was breaking a rule. Rules that apply only after the tour has started, however, can be presented graciously—and with a smile—by the guide. The requirement that a group remain together, refrain from touching furnishings, and not sit on furniture can be announced at the beginning of the tour, or even later, without causing embarrassment.

Procedures for sites open to the public. In addition to rules covering visitor behavior, the historic site should develop policies and standard procedures relating to the conducting of tours at each site. Such things as the following should be specified:

Numbers in groups

Where visitors enter and exit

Where interpreters will stand in each area

Traffic pattern and sequence in which rooms or areas will be shown

How interpreters will rotate assignments, if applicable

What points of emphasis should be made in each room or area

What responsibilities the interpreter has in each area

When interpreters will have rest break, lunch periods, etc.

Rules for interpreters. In addition to rules that apply to visitors and tours, a historic site should develop rules for interpreters. These rules should be reasonable and, under special circumstances, flexible. The individual interpreter should not decide whether he is going to follow a rule. It is assumed that he knew the rules under which he would work before he took the job. It is also assumed that there are good reasons for these rules. Only under emergency circumstances should the rules be suspended and even then, except in very unusual cases, they should be suspended only with the consent of the administration.

Rules for interpreters may include some or all of the following provisions:

1. Interpreters will park in spaces designated "Employees Only." The area closest to the historic site is to be left for visitors.

2. Interpreters will report to work at least ten minutes before the opening hour, completely ready to begin work. If an emergency makes it necessary for an interpreter to be late, he will notify his supervisor.

3. Interpreters will remain on duty until the historic site closes.

4. Interpreters will not leave the historic site during visiting hours without special permission from the staff member in charge.

5. Interpreters will not smoke nor eat except in the staff lounge, and especially not in front of guests.

6. Interpreters will not read nor write letters in front of visitors.

7. Interpreters may do handwork while they are temporarily off duty, but only when it does not interfere with the attention they should be paying the guests.

8. Interpreters will not use alcohol nor drugs before or during working hours.

9. Interpreters will not accept tips from guests. Non-monetary gifts of modest value sent by grateful guests may be accepted.

10. Interpreters will not correct other staff members in front of visitors.

11. Interpreters will always be appropriately groomed when they are on duty.

12. Off-duty interpreters will not talk in loud voices among themselves.

13. An off-duty interpreter in costume or uniform, even

away from the historic site, must remember that he represents the site to the public and should behave accordingly.

Emergency Procedures

In addition to rules insuring that visitors will tour the historic site in as comfortable a way as possible, provision should be made in advance for such emergencies as accidents and illnesses, fire, theft, and damage to the collection. Emergency procedures should be committed to memory by each interpreter; the correctness with which they are carried out affects both the welfare of guests and the legal liability of the site itself.

Illnesses and accidental injuries. Occasionally a visitor to a historic site will faint, become ill, or be accidentally injured during a tour. Interpreters should use the following procedures:

General Directions for Accidents or Illness

1. Make the visitor as comfortable as possible. Do not attempt first aid, unless you have had first aid training. If you have, do the following:
   a. *Give urgently necessary first aid when there is:*
      Severe bleeding
      Stoppage of breathing where cardiopulmonary resuscitation would help
      Poisoning—call the hospital
   b. *Keep the victim lying down*
      Protect from unnecessary handling and disturbance.
      Use caution when placing blankets under or on the patient.
   c. *Four basic life-saving steps:*
      Stop the bleeding
      Clear the air-passageway
      Treat for shock
      Treat the wound
      IF, IN YOUR JUDGMENT, AN AMBULANCE IS NEEDED, CALL THE RESCUE SQUAD (Telephone number)

N.B. The administration should provide first aid training for guides if they are to use anything but the simplest first aid procedures.[1]

2. Enlist the aid of another interpreter to call a doctor or the rescue squad if the illness or accident appears serious. The person conducting the tour should remain with the group while another person takes over the care of the ill or injured vistor.

3. Make a full report of the incident to the administration, including the nature of the illness or accident, the condition of the area in which an accident occurred, what was done for the injured person, and the attitude of the person involved.(A person is often embarrassed over a fall and will refuse to give a name. This fact should be noted in the report.)

4. Never tell visitors that a certain area is dangerous. If an injury should occur, such an admission might result in a lawsuit charging the historic site with negligence. Ask them to watch their step, or to note a landing or rough spot; and walk slowly yourself. While visitors are climbing or descending stairs, their attention should not be distracted by comments about objects they are passing.

5. If an accident occurs, do not tell guests that it is the fault of the historic site or that the historic site will pay all the medical costs, even if your insurance covers the situation. The liability for accidents is a legal matter.

The accident report form on the following page was developed by Colonial Williamsburg, but could be used by any historic site, large or small.

Fire. The gravest threat to historic sites is fire. Not only do most historic structures contain large quantities of combustible materials, but both the sites and their furnishings are, of course, unique and irreplaceable. Every staff member, therefore, must

---

1. Based on "Emergency Procedures," an unpublished manuscript developed by Elliot W. Jayne, Director of Security and Safety, for Colonial Williamsburg Foundation, in 1972, and used with permission.

share in the over-all responsibility for preventing fires; and the site director must, in addition, plan for the detection and quick fighting of any fire that may occur. *Protecting Our Heritage*, a publication of the National Fire Protection Association in collaboration with the American Association for State and Local History, contains many useful suggestions about fire protection and detection. Some of the most important of them follow — with the strong recommendation that every historic site staff member read the entire book:

Fire Prevention

1. Be careful to dispose of cigarettes in an appropriate receptacle and be sure they are completely extinguished.
2. Be sure that all hot plates, coffeepots, electric heaters, and the like are unplugged when they are not in use. Be sure also that there is nothing flammable near such devices.
3. Report worn electrical cords or fixtures to the site director at once.

In Case of Fire

1. Get everyone out of the building immediately. Give instructions calmly, but with authority. Your main responsibility is the safety of guests and staff.
2. Call the fire department. (Be sure the telephone number is attached to the telephone.) Speak calmly, giving the correct details. Remember where you are!
3. Notify the site director.
4. If any time is left and if you will not endanger yourself, try to extinguish the fire. Know where every fire extinguisher at the site is located and know the appropriate method of extinguishing different types of fire. Your local Fire Marshal can advise you in advance on the types of fire.

ACCIDENT REPORT—VISITORS

DATE _____

NAME OF INJURED   AGE-ESTIMATE IF NECESSARY

HOME ADDRESS

LOCAL ADDRESS

EXACT LOCATION OF ACCIDENT   DATE AND TIME OF ACCIDENT

INJURED PERSON'S VERSION OF HOW ACCIDENT OCCURRED

NATURE AND EXTENT OF INJURIES IF APPARENT

PROPERTY DAMAGE SUSTAINED OR CLAIMED BY INJURED PERSON

DID INJURED PERSON RECEIVE FIRST AID   FROM WHOM?
TREATMENT AT THE SCENE OF THE ACCIDENT?
DID INJURED PERSON GO TO A HOSPITAL FOR EXAMINATION?   WHICH HOSPITAL?

NAMES AND ADDRESSES OF EYE-WITNESSES

1.

2.

3.

4.

DID ANYONE EXAMINE   DID ANY UNUSUAL OR APPARENTLY
SCENE OF THE ACCIDENT   UNSAFE CONDITIONS EXIST?

IF SO, DESCRIBE

DID YOU OR ANY OTHER EMPLOYEE ON THE SCENE OF THE ACCIDENT COMMENT
ON THE CAUSE OF THE ACCIDENT OR THE NATURE OR EXTENT OF THE INJURIES?

OF SO, WHAT WAS SAID AND BY WHOM?

REMARKS

BY: _____

SCENE OF ACCIDENT

WITNESS

DATA ON INJURED PERSON

An accident report form developed at Colonial Williamsburg

Theft or damage to the collection. Security experts report that there is a greater incidence of theft at historic sites nowadays than in the past. Potential thieves are becoming more and more aware of the value of museum collections. Many of them are expert at spotting objects of considerable value that can be converted into cash and at locating "fences" willing to pay good prices for these pieces.

The administration has the chief responsibility for preventing theft or damage to the collection. Many museums now have very sophisticated devices to prevent thievery, particularly during the hours when the exhibitions are not open to the public. These include hidden microphones, microwave and ultrasonic detectors, television monitors, and many other devices. A historic site would do well to consult experts on what needs protecting and what devices will answer the need.

Less sophisticated techniques will frequently suffice during the hours that the public is present. Every historic site should consider the following protective measures for its collection:

SECURITY MEASURES

1. Make use of natural barriers such as store counters, display cases that can be locked, and the like.

2. Use ropes across chairs and other furniture that is not to be sat upon.

3. Use barriers that will allow people to enter rooms far enough to see the entire room but not far enough to endanger furniture and furnishings. These barriers may be simple ropes attached to posts, plastic barriers that can be seen through, or iron-work that is no more than about four feet high. Floor-to-ceiling barriers detract from any exhibition and should be used only when it is impossible to keep lower barriers under frequent surveillance.

4. Place all small, easily concealed objects beyond the reach of visitors.

5. Wire down small objects that can be picked up by guests.

6. If people are to walk through a room, use incon-

spicuous rope barriers to keep them away from articles that could be easily damaged or stolen.

7. Station security personnel in strategic places to help interpreters in the surveillance of guests, particularly when groups are large. These may be police guards or interpretive personnel especially assigned for this purpose.

Responsibility of Interpreters

Security for the collection of the historic site is usually the responsibility of an interpreter who is conducting a group of visitors through the site. He should follow these procedures:

PROCEDURES: INTERPRETERS

1. Check to see that everyone who enters an exhibit is properly ticketed. Unknown persons without tickets should be required to identify themselves. (If the entire exhibit is behind impenetrable barriers and the public is allowed to wander at will, this precaution, of course, is unnecessary.)

2. At the beginning of a tour, create a sense of respect for the collection as an irreplaceable part of our heritage which should be preserved for the permanent enjoyment and edification of this and future generations. Emphasize historical, not monetary, value. Discussion of costs not only is in bad taste, but an invitation to potential thieves who may return later to challenge the security system.

3. Also at the beginning of the tour, caution visitors about not handling furnishings. Such expressions as "When you see this fine collection of irreplaceable antiques, I am sure you will understand why we ask you not to sit or to handle objects as we go through this exhibition" will be inoffensive to visitors.

4. If people persist in handling objects or sitting where they are not supposed to be, remind them again as tactfully as possible so as not to embarrass them before the entire group. Such expressions as "I'm sorry, I must have forgotten

to tell you not to handle the furnishings. They are very rare, as I am sure you realize," or "I know it is a temptation to handle this, but when I remind you how very old it is, you will understand why we ask you not to," will minimize embarrassment to a person who has run his hand over a piece of delicate wallpaper or thoughtlessly picked up a priceless object. (The actual concealment of an object, of course, is a different matter. More on that later.)

5. Keep everyone in view while they are looking at an exhibit, particularly if they are clustered around a particular object. Before leaving for another area, be sure that the entire group is with you and that they all move at the same time. It is helpful to start talking about something they are about to see in order to get their attention and to have them all assembled before making the move.

6. If you see someone handling an object, ask him politely to replace it. Never accuse a visitor of stealing: Leave that to the police. (The laws of various states differ as to the legal liability you may incur by accusing a person of theft unless he has actually carried the object out of the building.)

7. If you know that a theft has actually occurred, report it to the person in charge of the building, who will call the police. (Be sure the telephone number is handy.) If possible, try to delay the suspect until the police arrive, but do not exert force to do this. Above all, be sure to get a good description of the suspect—what he is wearing, distinguishing features, transportation, and the like.

8. If someone has damaged an object, report this to the person in charge so that he can investigate the situation, and call the police if necessary. Never accuse a person of deliberately damaging an object. Again, let the police take care of that if necessary. (If a small child has either picked up an object or damaged something of value, it is legitimate to speak to the parents about keeping the child under control.)

9. In every instance where objects have been damaged or stolen, or there has been a attempt to steal them, make a full

written report of the incident. This can be done by written memorandum, or on a form created for that purpose:

INCIDENT REPORT

Incident: _____ Reporting Officer: _____ Date _____

Complainant:

    Name: _____ Address: _____ Phone: _____

    Place of Employment: _____ Local Address: _____

Victim:

Name: _____ Address: _____ Phone: _____

    Local Address: _____ Birth Date: _____

Witness:

    Name: _____ Address: _____ Phone: _____

    Local Address: _____

Suspect:

    Name: _____ Address: _____ Phone: _____

    Local Address: _____ Place of Employment: _____ Race: ____

    Sex: ____ Birth Date: ____ Height: ____ Weight: ____ Hair: ____

    Eyes: _____ Clothing: _____ Other Identifying Features: _____

Loss (description & estimated value):

Complete Details of What Happened:

Action Taken by Officer:

                        Approved by: _____

The responsibility of interpreters for the safeguarding of the site and its contents is important, but it must be kept in proper perspective. Security should be an ever-present concern, but not to the point that the role of police officer overwhelms the effectiveness of the interpretation. Without security, there would soon be nothing to interpret; and without interpretation, there would soon be no one who cared about what was saved.

After the site organization has considered carefully the procedures it will need to follow in conducting its tours and in providing for the security and safety of its visitors and its collections, it should put procedures in writing. It is important that this be done so that both new and older employees will know how to react in emergency situations and so that procedures do not break down because of word-of-mouth transmission from one interpreter to another.

10

Evaluation

THE success of an interpretation program must be measured,
not in terms of the interpreter, but in terms of the audience he is
trying to reach. No matter how diligently we have tried to apply
the very best techniques of interpretation, no matter how much
we may have been praised by professional associates, the measure of successful interpretation is the degree to which we have
created understanding in the mind and heart of the visitor, the
degree to which we somehow have communicated to him the
understanding we wish him to have of our site.

It is essential, at some step of the interpretive process, to
evaluate what visitors are getting from a visit to the site. What
impressions are they receiving that one may or may not wish to
give? What can the visitor tell us about administrative success
or failure in the management of the property? Why did the
visitor come to the site in the first place? Did he find there what
he expected? More? Less?

Personal interviews. There are a number of ways in which to
approach the evaluation of visitors to a site. The most expensive, but perhaps the most effective, in the long run, is the
combination of on-site and postvisit personal interviews. This
procedure begins with the development of a questionnaire that
becomes the basis of an on-site interview. Through this procedure an attempt is made to find out important facts about the
visitor: How old is he? How much education does he have?
Where does he live? These questions begin to give some understanding of the success of tourist promotion efforts. They also
begin to give a profile of the kind of person most often attracted
to the site and of effective ways to orient the interpretive program. Why did the visitor come to the site? Was it our promo-

tion? Word of mouth? Newspaper publicity? Is it a first visit, or has he been with us before? If a return visit, what can we learn about his reasons for coming again? What did he expect to receive the second time that he did not receive the first? Next, we may wish to ascertain what he has learned during his visit. What impressed him? What has he disliked or liked about the visit? What does he think the purpose of the site is? What message, if any, does he think we are trying to give him?

Some weeks, or even months, after his visit we should ask other questions of the same visitor. What does he *now* remember of the visit? What does he *now* think our purpose is? What new knowledge or understanding does he *now* believe he gained from the visit? What does he think was most interesting at the site? What does he remember as unpleasant or unsatisfying from the visit?

A survey in this depth requires considerable financial investment. Someone must conduct the first interview, which is at the site; and somehow we must conduct a second interview in which we must talk to the visitor where he resides. A plentitude of funds will help considerably in such an evaluation, but this is not the only way. It is possible, for example, to conduct the on-site interview through the use of volunteers who have received some training in the procedures of interviews. The questions to be asked should be developed with the help of someone trained in marketing survey techniques to eliminate ambiguities and elicit the objective answers needed for improvement. Such a person should also be helpful in developing the interview techniques. We do not want to ask the kind of questions, for example, that encourage either favorable or unfavorable responses. The way in which questions are asked can determine the kind of response. We should try to get the most objective response, not the response we might like to receive.

Professional marketing survey firms are an excellent source of help in planning your own survey, particularly if they have some experience with cultural institutions. Such firms may be too expensive, however, for low-budget sites. If that is your problem, there are several alternatives. A local university with courses in marketing may be willing—even anxious—to use your survey needs as a class project, with expenses limited to the printing costs of the questionnaire itself. The marketing department of a local business firm may be willing to help. Regardless of the way you do it, the survey is no better than the questionnaire and the interview techniques, so get help and do it right.

Conducting the postvisit interviews is more difficult than those on-site. If we can afford to send a trained interviewer to the home of the visitor, we should do so. If we cannot—and this will be the case with most sites—we should explore the possibilities of conducting the interview by phone. A careful check of larger business firms in the area may turn up one that has leased long distance (WATS) lines. Should this be the case, there may be a possibility of using those lines outside of regular business hours for a telephone survey of previous visitors to the site. Telephone interviews, of course, shield the interviewee from personal contact with the interviewer, but that need not be a handicap. In many circumstances, the anonymity afforded by the phone will encourage the respondent to speak more frankly than would be the case on a person-to-person basis.

If the telephone cannot be used, the alternative will be to mail follow-up questionnaires to former visitors and hope for an adequate return. If this is done, be sure that the questionnaires are as brief as possible and are easy to answer. A questionnaire that can be checked and returned (in a furnished, self-addressed, stamped envelope) is much more likely to be answered than a questionnaire that, no matter how complete and information-seeking, is so complex that only the most dedicated (or otherwise idle) visitor will take the time to respond.

Observations at the site. Despite the development of printed questionnaire and interview techniques, many professionals maintain that the best way to evaluate the effectiveness of the interpretive program is still observation of the visitor by the historic site staff. Some organizations, as a routine matter, insist that employees in the interpretive division mingle—unnoticed, of course—with occasional groups of visitors in order to overhear visitor comments and observe the interpreter's work. Only in this way can the staff really know how long visitors remain before a given museum case; or how long people are willing to spend reading that new label that was so popular in the last staff meeting; or what kind of private comments visitors are making beyond the earshot of the interpreter; or what kinds of questions come up over and over again, indicating that some revision of the existing interpretation might make the interpreter's job easier.

Equally important is the exchange of ideas among interpreters and other staff members. No two employees view the interpretation in quite the same light. Administrative staff members may get something quite different out of the interpretive program, for example, than the curatorial staff. New ideas ought to be "bounced off" staff members, trustees, and members of the historical organization, not to give these other people a veto of the interpretive staff's work, but to get from them whatever ideas might improve the interpretation.

Analysis of letters. Another useful way to evaluate the interpretation is to review carefully all letters both of complaint and praise. Letters of praise offer clues as to what in an interpretation appeals to visitors and accomplishes our objectives. It is tempting, obviously, to bury or lose unfavorable letters in order to save embarrassment, but this is not a useful approach to the problem. Even the nuttiest of letter-writers may tell us something we had not perceived about the site we run; and the more intelligent letter-writers frequently suggest, if only by implication, means by which we might improve our interpretive efforts. Letters of complaint should be read by the director and by other staff members. No one person on the staff has a monopoly on insight; the more people who read and react to the complaint letters, the more chance we have of improving our performance.

Attendance figures. Finally, one of the accepted methods of evaluating performance is by studying the attendance figures. First, of course, it is necessary to be certain that the attendance figures are a true measure of the number of people who came to tour the site. All too often, reported attendance is an estimate, or is determined by a traffic counter that also records large numbers of people who are there for other reasons than visiting the site—using the nearby road as a commuting shortcut or traveling it to reach the local lovers' lane. Attendance also is boosted at some sites by people seeking rest-room facilities. Sheer numbers will never measure the success of an educational effort, but attendance figures do give some indication of success in promoting visitation; they may also indicate favorable word-of-mouth reputation; and often they can tell us how successful we have been in persuading local people to make return visits with their friends.

The success of any evaluation program rests most of all on how honest we are in assessing our accomplishments. The most sophisticated and expensive audience survey is worthless if we refuse to learn from its findings. Interpretation is far from an exact science. It is made up of inspiration, research, dedication to a worthy cause, and commitment to an audience that seeks us out and attempts to share with us the excitement, the rewards, and the understanding that we who run the sites count as the personal rewards of our involvement. As interpreters, we face the strongest possible challenge to awaken in others an appreciation, an understanding, a perspective on the accomplishments of generations now departed. We will not meet that challenge solely by satisfying ourselves. We will do so only by reaching beyond our own circle of fellow-believers in history to a general public that must be sold over and over again on the proposition that history is their collective memory, the record, not just of man's failures, but of his accomplishments, not just of great leaders, but of the many followers, not just of mansions, but of subdivision houses, and of small farms, and of inner-city slums.

Because we appreciate and have some understanding of the past, we are privileged to serve as trustees for it. To the degree that we serve others rather than being self-serving, that we interpret to others rather than talking to ourselves, that we help our visitors to glimpse the deeper meaning of the sites in our custody, we shall have met the enormous responsibility we have, not only to our own generation, but to generations yet unborn.

About the Appendices

The authors debated at some length about appendix material for this book: when we completed the first draft of the manuscript, we were startled to find that there was almost as much material in the section we were calling "Appendices" as there was in the manuscript itself—a situation we promptly resolved (over the next several months!) by a considerable amount of rewriting, deleting, and tightening.

After still further consideration, we decided to include as appendices as graphic an account as we could assemble of the way an interpretation of a historic site evolves—a recognizable, step-by-step, how-it-can-be-done approach. We offer this material in the hope that newcomers to the profession may find it helpful and that old hands will take the time to let us know wherein such sample guidelines can be improved.

Appendix 1 takes a newly formed group through the entire process of acquiring a site, setting up administrative procedures, hiring personnel, organizing volunteers, presenting the site, and evaluating further needs for better presentation. Appendix 2 is a fully developed model interpretation, closely keyed to the tour guidelines set up in Appendix 1. The purpose of including both, of course, is not merely to expound on facts already given, but to show concretely how a brief topical outline can be filled in and fleshed out, following an outline form.

A personal note: Dr. William B. Southard was a real person. He was the great-grandfather of co-author Shirley Low, and actual facts from his life are included in this material.

The Authors

Appendix 1

Decisions Made in Saving a Historic House

With the town of Riverton growing, new businesses moving in, and a large shopping area proposed for location in the heart of the old part of town, a group of citizens becomes concerned about the proposed bulldozing of the town's oldest, best-known Victorian house. Determined to save it if they can, they have to work fast. Many decisions must be made.

A committee is formed. Members weigh personal sentiment against the practicality of what they propose. Their first major decision is that the house is worth saving, for many reasons: it was built in the 1850s by Dr. William B. Southard, a medical doctor, distinguished professionally, admired by his contemporaries, a vital contributor to his community. The architectural style of the house reflects the tastes of more prosperous early settlers in this midwestern town. A bit elaborate for modern tastes, it was once the height of fashion in Riverton. Its location, near the junction of the canal and the river that provided the young town's early transportation, helps to illustrate considerations that early planners had to make. Its restoration will document for visitors the life of an early Riverton settler who made important contributions to the community.

Documentary evidence about the house and its owner must be evaluated. The committee is lucky: the same family has lived in the house since it was built, and they didn't throw things away. Most of the furnishings acquired by the Southards over the years are still there, including pieces the family proudly boasts have been in the family since before the Revolution. A more recent owner concedes that some of the fine pieces may go back to 1810, but not quite to pre-Revolutionary times. This man, genuinely interested in collecting, has checked family legends in authoritative reference books on antiques.

Stashed away in the attic in old trunks are family letters and diaries, including those kept by Dr. Southard when he worked his way through medical school by driving a mule along the canal, pulling barges to the river. His account books, too, are available, and contain evidence that the barter system was not unknown to the medical profession in the 1860s. The doctor's journal also carries a contemporary account of the founding of the Republican party at Jackson, Michigan, which Dr. Southard attended. Someone must be chosen to evaluate these documents. The committee may decide on an able, retired history teacher, or a young graduate student living in the community and working toward an advanced degree in architectural history; he would welcome the opportunity to study changes made in the old house as it was adapted to the tastes and comforts of successive owners.

The next major decision involves money: can the committee afford to acquire the house, restore it to its original appearance, and furnish it, either with original family pieces or with appropriate ones of the same period? The present owner, a great-grandson of the original builder, does not come to Riverton very often, these days; his family is scattered and not much interested in Riverton or the old family home. Perhaps he might be persuaded to give the old house to the city, or perhaps he would sell it cheaply. Having decided that the house is worth saving, committee members believe they can do it practically by getting enough citizens in the community interested—doctors, especially, might contribute, and members of the Republican party that Dr. Southard supported. Eventually, if the house is acquired, restored accurately, and presented attractively to the public, enough money from visitors' admissions fees may be realized to pay for its upkeep and for modest salaries to people who will serve as interpreters.

A third major decision is not to move the Southard house away from the encroachments of the proposed shopping center, much as committee members would like to avoid having modern structures impinge on the past. An important part of the structure's historical significance would be lost in taking it away from the junction of canal and river that says so much about why this particular site was selected for a town in the first place. They will leave it where it is, surrounded by the stately trees that Dr. Southard planted and the gardens he laid out. If enough funds are realized, they may even put back the orchard and, perhaps, eventually, the apiary. It should provide an interesting contrast for modern shoppers loading their grocery carts nearby.

Planning Interpretation

Initial decisions have been made and acted on, the house has been acquired, accurately restored, and authentically furnished. Much information has been accumulated about Dr. Southard from family letters and journals, from the state medical society that he helped to found and that he served as first president. There are newspaper accounts of his activities and those of his contemporaries. Old-timers in the area have been interviewed and their recollections of earlier years in Riverton recorded in an oral history project conducted by a professor from a nearby college. The best workable way to present this information to visitors must now be planned.

The original committee, now greatly enlarged by the addition of local history enthusiasts, antique collectors, and creative, interested youngsters and oldsters, realize that they cannot possibly tell visitors everything known about Dr. Southard, his era, and the styles of architecture and furnishings represented by his home. They must decide on the most valid points for interpreting the site.

First, they envision their probabley audience: realistically, they concede that probably not many people driving through the area on the interstate highway from distant places will delay their journey by getting off on narrow, meandering, local roads to visit the home of a man they never heard of in history books. Most visitors will probably be from the immediate area. Their motives will vary. Some local people may visit the house because the period it represents may seem glamorous. Older townspeople will recall that it wasn't all that glamorous, but they will enjoy the memory of the era it evokes. Younger people may be interested in the way their grandparents lived and intrigued by the differences between life then and now.

The committee must select information about Dr. Southard and his time that will be meaningful to at least a majority of these visitors— facts about the man, about what life was like in those days, about the tastes of the time, the prevailing architectural styles, and something of the area's early history. They set down a written guide to go by:

Facts about Dr. William B. Southard

Background
> Born in Clyde, New York, August 10, 1822; son of Isaac Southard, a farmer, and his wife, Susan Caryl; nephew of Samuel Lewis Southard, a member of James Monroe's cabinet.
>
> Married Hulda Jones; three daughters, Augusta, Ida, and Mary; one son, Dr. Eugene Southard.
>
> William's parents moved westward gradually and settled in Riverton in 1842.
>
> Died in Riverton, February 21, 1904.

Profession

Medical school, 1847-1850.

Practiced medicine for fifty-four years.

Founded state medical society, 1870.

Instrumental in improving medical education in the state.

Had young, aspiring doctors assist him, to improve their skills.

Tastes in Architecture, Furnishings, and Gardens

Built his home in the current (1850s) fashion, Gothic Revival.

Laid out extensive orchards, gardens in the naturalistic style of the period.

Furnished home with family pieces brought from New York State and the new-style, late-Victorian chairs and sofas, beds and dressers.

Importance of Dr. William B. Southard

Raised standards for the medical profession.

Helped found the Republican party. Strong supporter of Lincoln.

Helped improve educational opportunities for local children from poorer families.

Helped improve appearance of the city by planting trees, developing a public park along the river, donating his own land for that purpose. The park is still called Southard Park.

Beginning with basic facts, committee members ponder ways to impart certain concepts about the man and his era—things that they hope visitors will feel and appreciate, concepts not so concrete as the basic facts, including these points, which they add to the written guidelines:

This area was a land of opportunity for many who moved westward in the middle of the last century. They found a good life here.

Dr. Southard was a man concerned about his fellow man, and he left this place better than he found it.

Doctors endured much a hundred years ago.

The man was a real person, a human being, full of character and quirks, abilities and accomplishments.

Facts about the life of the time in that area are also added to the guidelines.

Facts about Riverton in Mid-Nineteenth Century

Family ties were very close in those days. Sometimes as many as four generations lived in the same house.

Children attended one-room schoolhouses, but they learned a lot. A number of them, including Dr. Southard's three daughters and one son, went on to college in a day when not many young women were considered college material. Education was important to the people in this town.

Parties were very informal—they included quilting bees, picnics, church suppers, ice-skating, and boating parties.

There were two major churches in Riverton, the Presbyterian and the Baptist; there was one dissident group that had broken away from the Baptist congregation. Families attended church as a group regularly. They were quite fundamental in their beliefs.

The taste of the time was reflected in ornate architecture and furnishings, elaborate iron fences around yards, naturalistic plantings in gardens, broad front lawns in front of houses. These styles reflected degrees of culture and affluence and represented good craftsmanship in which workmen took pride.

One goal of the proposed interpretation is to impart some understanding of the values of Riverton's past generations as indicated by the historical record and the tangible reminders of their life in this community. The committee's purpose is not to glamorize a simpler type of life, but they hope to show it as basically a good life.

Presenting the House to the Public

Aware that a list of unadorned facts about the man and identification of the furnishings of his house will not enable visitors to visualize the man or the era, the committee begins work on interpretive approaches.

Meantime, they work on practical procedures for showing visitors through the Southard house.

For staff, they plan to have at least one paid interpreter and several dozen volunteers.

For schedule, they decide to keep the house open from April through September, from 9:00 A.M. to 5:00 P.M. It is to open on time: many committee members have experienced the frustration of arriving at historic sites at which advertised hours of operation are not observed. During the winter, the house will open only for special events. There will be at least three interpreters on duty at all times. On days when heavy visitation is expected—after several months of keeping a tally of visitors, the staff can anticipate times when many people are likely to come—a couple of extra interpreters will be brought in from a group of volunteers.

Tour routing is planned. Tours will start in the old barn. Groups waiting for a tour to begin may view displays a local art teacher has planned. Some of the doctor's original letters, journals, and account books are on display, laminated, and in cases to protect them from humidity and heat. The cases have been donated by a Riverton doctor who, as a young man, was a great admirer of Dr. Southard and his work. In a way, the display is also a memorial to this man.

There is a small display of the findings of local amateur archaeologists from digs along the river: Indian arrowheads, fragments of cooking pots, bits of nineteenth-century pottery, part of an old leather saddle bag, the lock from a rifle probably carried in the Civil War, and a mysterious skull. These things are carefully arranged, with easy-to-read captions that explain clearly what the findings represent.

It is agreed that visitors will probably get more out of the tour if they are conducted all the way through house and grounds by the same person. That way, major points of interest may be made without repetition. So that all visitors may see the rooms, tour groups will be limited to ten. If visitation is heavy, an interpreter will be stationed in each room and crowds may go through on their own after a brief introduction before starting. At certain areas, interpretation will be given along the way. And of course visitors will be able to ask questions. A total traffic pattern is added to the guidelines:

I. *The Barn*

Visitors will be given a general introduction to Dr. Southard, the town in which he lived, and the type of life he lived.

II. *The Garden and Orchard*

Dr. Southard's love of nature will be mentioned as the group tours garden and orchard. Points stressed will be his love of planting trees, his apiary, and styles of gardens popular in the 1860s.

III. *The Front Yard and the House*

On the lawn, facing the house, the interpreter will discuss the building's style of architecture, the era's prevalent use of cast-iron fences, cast-iron deer, and circular raised flower gardens with brick boundaries.

The importance of the canal and the river to the town will fit in at this stage.

IV. *The Doctor's Office*

Visitors will enter the house through the east front door to

Dr. Southard's office, where they will learn about his contribution to the medical profession, his education and influence, his career. The types of instruments and medications he used will be presented, as will a description of what doctoring was like in the late nineteenth century.

V. *The Library*

Guests may look into the library just back of Dr. Southard's office. Pertinent at this point will be an explanation of the type of books popular at that time, the doctor's professional library, and the education of the children.

VI. *The Parlor*

In the parlor, visitors will learn about the use of the room for special guests such as the preacher, special occasions such as weddings or funerals, and for family prayers. They will also learn something of the religious beliefs of that time, the social life of the family, and the styles of furnishings then popular.

VII. *The Sitting Room*

Visitors move across the hall to the west front room, on the opposite side of the house from the office. There they will hear about the size of the family, group activities in the sitting room, and the use of the furnishings. Dr. Southard's interest in politics may be mentioned here.

VIII. *The Downstairs Bedroom*

Visitors will be led out into the hall again and back to the downstairs bedroom. Here, they may learn about the era's usual facilities for bathing, the custom of having children born at home in beds—such as the rather bulky one here— and of the custom of retiring and rising early. Before the hearty breakfasts could be prepared, fires had to be got going and the horses fed.

IX. *The Front West Bedroom*

Into the hall again and up the stairs to the bedroom over the sitting room, the group may be told about children and grandchildren. The furnishings will be explained, especially the hair wreath.

X. *Eugene's Room*

Visitors move next down the side hall, past the two other front bedrooms, stopping at the room of the doctor's son Eugene, whose short career as a doctor and whose early death may be mentioned.

XI. *The Dining Room*

The group next moves back through the side hall to the main

hall and down the stairs to the dining room, where they will be told about the eating customs of the time and the styles of dishes and silver used.

XII. *The Kitchen and Pantry*

Next stops are the kitchen and pantry. Visitors will learn here about vegetables and fruits available from the family's garden, about the storage of food, cooking and baking, and canning. Hot gingerbread will be served fresh from the oven of the wood stove, with homemade cider. Visitors will be seated outside in the garden during good weather; in bad weather, they will be seated around a large kitchen table.

Seeking the best aid they can get for their new interpreters, the committee decide that they need a carefully planned, well-thought-out model interpretation by a capable writer who is also familiar with the house and the area. Once again, they are lucky: a Mrs. McConkey who lives in Riverton is a writer, is interested in historic sites, and her occasional newspaper feature stories about historic sites and person-alities are well received. The committee asks her to write the sample interpretation. It appears separately, as Appendix 2, following these pages.

The Education and Training of Interpreters

The committee—which has now become the Southard Memorial Foundation—is delighted to have Mrs. McConkey's model interpreta-tion. They feel that the anecdotes about the doctor and his family will make them all more real to the visiting public. They agree that the use of the entire house and furnishings helps to show a way of life of the last half of the nineteenth century and the aesthetic tastes of the time more fully than merely presenting the identification of furniture styles would.

Interpretation of the house would be fairly easy if the interpreters could simply say what is in the model, and nothing else. Visitors are curious, however; they ask a lot of questions, some of which the interpreters cannot answer, and they also want to pursue extensively some points made by interpreters.

Having interviewed a number of prospects, the Foundation have selected as a paid Supervisor of Interpreters a college-educated woman, recently widowed. A former history teacher, she has worked during the summers at a well-known historic site as a guide. She is interested in antiques; she has traveled extensively; she has poise, intelligence, and a friendly personality, works well with people, and she seems well informed about a variety of subjects. They outline her responsibilities:

SUPERVISOR OF INTERPRETERS

Responsibilities

The Southard Memorial Foundation will set policy for the interpretation of the Southard House and for procedures to be used by the interpreters. Following guidelines set by the Foundation, the Supervisor of Interpreters will have the following responsibilities:

Help to recruit and interview prospective interpreters.

Prepare new interpreters to work at the Southard House, enlisting the help of experts when needed.

Make work schedules for all interpreters.

Be responsible for finding substitutes for interpreters who cannot work at the time scheduled.

Supervise interpreters on the job in the house.

Observe interpretation and hold conferences concerning performance.

Participate in interpreting the house part of the time.

Confer with the Southard Memorial Foundation periodically on the progress of interpreters in presenting the house and on personnel problems. The supervisor will have authority to handle such problems according to his or her best judgment.

The Supervisor of Interpreters will set up a training library of books, film strips, slides, and mimeographed research reports for the interpreters. He or she will enlist the help of experts in further research on the family, the period of history involved, architectural details, gardens, and furnishings.

The Supervisor of Interpreters will be responsible for keeping track of the numbers of visitors to the house each day and will supervise the sale of tickets, checking and depositing the money taken in from ticket sales, brochures, and post cards.

The Supervisor of Interpreters will work five days a week. On the other two days, a volunteer will be assigned to fill in as Supervisor of Interpreters.

A workshop on managing and interpreting historic sites is to be held soon in the area. The Foundation decides to send their Supervisor of Interpreters to the workshop, to learn from professionals how to handle the position.

A group of women are eager to work as volunteers on a part-time basis. Three have young children in school, so that they will be able to work during school hours, particularly with school groups, who usually come during that time. There also are two retired military officers interested in spending a few hours a week at the house, especially on weekends. Several widows have expressed a desire to participate, as well. And during the summer, when the staff must be increased considerably, a few of the local teachers are willing to work part-time at the house. The Foundation would prefer a regular paid staff of at least four well-qualified people, but there is enough local interest in the site to staff the house adequately, though scheduling is more difficult with the odd hours a number of the volunteers can work.

It is hard to resist every offer made to be a volunteer, but standards must be kept as high as possible, so the Foundation rejects those who lack the necessary qualifications. Tactfully, they steer some applicants to other necessary activities, such as typing research information, cataloging the collection, and selling post cards and brochures about the house.

The unpaid interpreters have organized themselves into the William B. Southard Volunteers, with the purpose of getting to know each other better and of learning as much as they can about their project. Membership in the Volunteers is becoming something of a status symbol.

Qualified as most of the new staff may be, they cannot possibly know all the answers to questions that will be asked, and they need additional information to substantiate the information they give in interpreting Dr. Southard's house. The Foundation decides to enlist the help of someone with extensive experience in helping to train interpreters at a much larger site. They cannot afford an extensive training program, but they feel that new interpreters will benefit from some additional background training. Following the advice of the consultant, a committee of the Foundation works out plans with the Supervisor of Interpreters for special classes on the Southard family; medical practices of the nineteenth century; midwestern life in the nineteenth century—cooking, games, education, religion (with special attention to the beliefs of Presbyterians and Baptists), eating customs, and the like; architectural styles of that period; styles of furniture, ceramics, fabrics, lighting, and so on; styles of gardens, with lists of flowers, trees, and vegetables; political issues; how to interpret a historic site effectively; and safety and security.

The Supervisor of Interpreters, following the suggestions of the professional adviser, has planned an education program, using questions for the interpreters, with specific references in books and mimeographed research reports around which class discussions will be held. She herself has done extensive research, so that she will be able to fill in most of the gaps that the volunteers have not covered. The interpreters should be able to answer most of the questions likely to be asked. A file of questions frequently asked and their answers will be kept. The interpreters also should be able to speak with some authority on most subjects covered in interpretation of the house.

One of the most challenging parts of the program suggested by the professional consultant is a demonstration by the Supervisor of Interpreters of the way the house is to be interpreted and visitors taken care of. The supervisor, not sure that she is *that* qualified, discovers that she not only enjoys doing a demonstration, but that it really is helpful to new interpreters.

The interpreters soon recognize that, although they can never know all there is to be known about the site they help to present, they can steadily learn more about the people, the period of history, the artifacts, and other aspects of it. They are encouraged to study on their own, selecting topics of special interest to themselves, and share their findings with fellow volunteers.

The consultant on historic sites has suggested that, during the season when the house is not open regularly, the interpreters might get together with interpreters from similar sites within a radius of seventy miles to hold advanced classes on topics studied in their beginning classes. She suggests professors from the nearby university who will talk to the combined group on their specialty and local architects who might be willing to speak on the favorite styles of the period. Local ministers usually welcome a chance to explain what their churches believe. The garden club can provide speakers on garden styles, and the local art museum has specialists on the decorative arts.

Some of these authorities who have to travel some distance may ask a small fee, but the majority will probably settle for travel expenses.

Four historic sites in the area get together and recruit specialists for training classes during a three-week period in February and March. Classes will meet in the Southard barn. The program is well planned and worthwhile:

ADVANCED TRAINING FOR THE RIVERTON AREA
HISTORIC SITES INTERPRETERS

February 24   *Life in the Riverton Area in the Nineteenth Century*
Dr. Dorothy C. Scott, State University History Department

February 26   *Political Issues in the United States, 1850-1900*
              Prof. Marston Balch, State University Government
              Department
February 28   *Role of Women in the United States in the Nine-*
              teenth Century
              Miss Melinda Tanis, Riverton High School
March 3   *Nineteenth-Century Garden Styles*
              Mrs. Mildred Dunn, Riverton Garden Club
March 5   *Furniture Styles of the Nineteenth Century*
              Allen Morton, Curator, Art Museum
March 7   *Religious Movements of the Nineteenth Century*
              The Rev. Martin Simmons, Pastor, First Presbyterian
              Church
March 10   *The History of Medicine: Nineteenth-Century Dis-*
              coveries and Practices
              Dr. Rush McNair III, Riverton
March 12   *Architectural Styles in the Riverton Area in the Nine-*
              teenth Century
              (Meet at the Courthouse for walking tour of Riverton's
              oldest section)
March 14   *Education in the Nineteenth Century*
              Prof. Ernest Stetson, Professor Emeritus of Education,
              State University

The Supervisor of Interpreters at the Southard House made reading materials suggested by discussion leaders available to participants in the training programs.

Appendix 2

Model Interpretation:
The Dr. William B. Southard House

[Tour of house and gardens will take about 45 minutes.] *The Barn* (5-7 minutes) [Interpreter stands facing the door in the center of the barn.]

Welcome to Dr. William B. Southard's home. If you had visited Dr. Southard about a century ago, you well might have come to the barn first, because more than likely you would have driven over dusty dirt roads in a horse-drawn buggy. One of Dr. Southard's hired men would have stabled your horse while you made your way to the doctor's office at the front of the house or to the parlor just opposite the office. If you were not staying long, you might have tied your horse to that iron hitching post that you passed as you came in.

The Southards had lots of company. Both the doctor and his wife were well liked in the community and frequently had as house guests friends and relatives from back home in New York State, as well as local people who dropped in for a sociable cup of tea. And, of course, the doctor had many patients, because he was the only doctor in this area for several years. And with three attractive daughters and a handsome son, there were plenty of young people around.

The buggy and sleigh in front of you belonged to Dr. Southard. One contemporary doctor recalled that the local banker once asked, "Did you ever notice how Dr. Southard sits forward on the very edge of his buggy seat, thinking he will get there a foot or fourteen inches sooner?" The same doctor described Dr. Southard in later years as "short and pudgy and much outworn. He walked with very short steps and with a stumbling gait."[1]

Dr. Rush McNair, who as a young medical student spent a lot of time learning from him, recalled: "All of Dr. Southard's fifty-four years of

---

1. This quotation and the other anecdotes appearing as quotations here appeared originally in an article by Dr. Rush McNair in the *Kalamazoo* (Michigan) *Gazette*, March 14, 1937, and are used by permission of the publisher.

practice were during those long, wearisome horse-and-buggy and horse-and-sleigh days. And he worked hard, continuing up to two days before his death." Dr. McNair also recalled: "One bitter cold night, as late as 1875, there was a loud knocking at the door about midnight and as Dr. Southard answered it, a man said: The wife of the man I work for is awful sick. I guess she's going to die, and he sent me down to get you.' The doctor hurriedly dressed, and they started the eight-mile drive over roads that were almost impassable. Twice during the trip the sleigh turned over and dumped them out, and it was nearly 4:00 A.M. when, nearly frozen, they reached their destination. When they went inside, the husband said: Well, you've been so long coming, my wife's better, now, and of course I can't pay you for the visit, because she's pulling through without any medicine.' "

You may know that Dr. Southard was the son of a farmer, Isaac Southard, and his wife, the former Susan Caryl. They were living on a farm near Clyde, New York, when William was born. The family moved westward, staying for a short time in Angola, Indiana, before moving on to a farm near Riverton in 1842. Riverton was a tiny settlement at that time, with only about a hundred people living here. Even in 1865, when Dr. Southard's oldest daughter, Augusta, was eleven, the town still did not have a telegraph station. Augusta remembered getting all dressed up to visit the nearest large city and driving into town, to find all of the stores closed and the streets draped in black bunting. It was only then that they found out that President Abraham Lincoln had been shot in Washington three days before.

Dr. Southard loved to recount that, under the oaks at Jackson, Michigan, he had helped to form the Republican party. He was a great supporter of Lincoln and the new party, much to the horror of some of his Democrat friends and relatives.

Riverton might have been small, but it had promise, situated as it is, right where the canal meets the river. That would eventually be a big economic boost for the community.

William's father rather hoped that William would be a preacher or a lawyer, or even a farmer, as he was. He couldn't understand why William wanted to be a doctor.

The town of Riverton was glad of that, however, because he was a good doctor, one they could depend on, and he did much to improve his profession. He also helped to beautify his town. He is remembered with affection by old-timers even today.

William married Hulda Jones in 1852, two years after he set up practice. At the same time, he built the house you are about to visit. The house has been owned by his descendants until recently, when retired Ambassador John C. Bloom, Dr. Southard's great-grandson, deeded it to the Southard Memorial Foundation to keep it open to the public.

We are fortunate in having such original documents as you see in these cases to give us information about Dr. Southard, his family, and about life in Riverton more than a hundred years ago. Most of the period furnishings in the house are family pieces that either have been in the house all these years or are on permanent loan to the Memorial Foundation by interested friends or descendants.

I am going to show you the gardens and orchards as we approach Dr. Southard's office. I must ask you to stay together as a group. You may take pictures as you tour the house, but please do not use the type of flash bulbs that might explode. When you see the fine collection of irreplaceable furnishings in the house, I am sure that you will understand why we ask you not to sit on any of the chairs or sofas and not to handle any of the objects on display. My name is _____; please don't hesitate to ask questions as we go along.

The Garden and the Orchard (3-4 minutes) [Interpreter stands near the vegetable garden. In case of bad weather, talk about the garden and canal in the barn. Lead the group directly to the office.]

Dr. Southard may have rejected his father's hope that he might be a farmer, if not a preacher or a lawyer, but he never lost what a contemporary called "his love of Nature and Nature's God." When he could, he would steal away from his office or from rounds over the country roads caring for the sick, to visit his orchards, his apiary, and his vineyard. One of his friends said about him: "There, with his feet upon the good earth, his body and his arteries and nerves lost their tension. There he breathed a different air from that of the sick room and Nature gave him her vitality and his perennial rebirths of life."

Some people condemned Dr. Southard for leaving his office often to work on his orchard, but one doctor, who as a boy had known Dr. Southard, defended him: "He was more natural, sweeter, and cleaner and lived a score of years longer than those who, twenty-four hours a day, without cessation, mingled with fevers and chills, constipation and diarrhea, diseases of the urinary system, fits, malingerers, and ungrateful responses to services rendered."

His greatest relaxation was to trim and graft apple trees. He loved all trees, and perhaps—next to the fruit trees—elms and chestnuts were his favorites. He planted them, not only all over his own property, but all over town. People asked, "William, why do you persist in planting trees? You won't live to enjoy them." He always responded seriously, "Somebody will." And Riverton is still a lovely, tree-shaded town.

You will notice that the gardens, which have been replanted here, reflect the styles of the 1850s and 1860s, an era of large lawns, informal plantings in flower beds, and a vegetable garden close to the kitchen door, providing fresh vegetables during the growing season and others, such as rutabagas, parsnips, potatoes, and carrots, for storage in the root cellar built into that mound near the kitchen door.

You will notice that the barn is set back from the house quite a distance. I suppose the odor of manure was the reason. They did not waste that valuable commodity. It was piled behind the barn for what people in those days called "taking the heat," before being spread as fertilizer on the gardens. The watering trough will be familiar to many of you who were brought up on farms.

Dr. Southard may have regretted building his barn so far from the house. The family used to chuckle over his experience of walking in his sleep one bitter cold night and awakening to find himself at the barn door, surrounded by two feet of snow in every direction. He didn't talk about how it felt to get back to the house, barefooted and dressed only in his long nightshirt. Family legend maintains that he was still embarrassed about the incident years later.

Some of you may remember a well like this at your grandparents' house. Try it, if you like. You simply turn the handle and let the oaken bucket descend—gently—into the water below. Hear the splash? Then you reverse the turn of the handle and bring the bucket full of water to the top of the well. [Let a child do this.] It is fun to do once or twice, perhaps; but if you were completely dependent on drawing all your water for drinking, bathing, washing clothes, and everything else, it might not be so much fun. You can understand why Hulda Southard was delighted when her husband installed a real pump. Her grandchildren recall that she always kept a bucket of water handy to prime the pump when the water did not flow as it should. They thought it was fun to pump water—it probably was fun, since they did not have to do it several times a day.

You will notice that the original pergola is still standing, with grapevines over it, as it was in Dr. Southard's time.

Let us walk to the front of the house now for a good look at the canal.

The Front Yard (3-4 minutes) [Interpreter stands on the bluff overlooking the locks where the canal enters the river.]

The locks make it possible for barges to descend into the river and continue down the river to the Gulf. It is easy to see why Riverton was founded here, and why the river traffic brought prosperity to this community. With this view, it is obvious, too, why Dr. Southard built his home at this particular spot.

His father before him had sent many a bargeful of apples along the canal from his home back east to the ports farther down the river. He came with one load, himself, once, and decided that Riverton would be a good place to live. He purchased farm land just east of the city and brought his family here, shipping most of his household goods by barge and driving overland in a Conestoga wagon.

William himself had interesting memories of the canal, for, as a young man, he earned his way through medical school by driving a mule that pulled barges along the canal. You can still see a bit of the path through the trees, if you look over the bluff. In the house, you will see William's old wooden chest in which he kept clothes and books on the barge. Legend says that the mule knew the path so well that William could study his medical books as he walked or rode along.

With the coming of the railroad and airplanes, the canal and river are not so important to the area economically now as they were a century ago. In those days, Riverton developed as a trading center, particularly for the transportation of fruit and coal.

In the summer, the townspeople used to have picnics along the canal and they went fishing and boating on the river. The canal usually was frozen over, most of the winter, and made an ideal skating rink for the young men. It was thought not quite proper for young ladies to ice-skate, so, when Dr. Southard's young daughters, Augusta, Ida, and Mary, returned from visiting relatives back east, they shocked the local townspeople here by being the first young ladies to ice-skate—a skill they had learned from their cousins back in New York State. It was also fun to cut holes through the ice and fish. Some even constructed small wooden shelters to protect themselves from the cold wind.

Just to the left, you can see the city park developed on land that Dr. Southard gave for that purpose. It is still called Southard Park.

The cast-iron fence around the large front yard was the height of fashion, a hundred years ago, and nearly everybody who was anybody had cast-iron deer, such as those, on their lawns. Fragments of bricks were unearthed here, in a circle, indicating that there was a round, raised flower garden at this spot. People used to call this type of encircling brick "batterboards." The garden has been restored to its late-nineteenth-century appearance.

As we approach the house, we see a structure typical of the Gothic Revival style. Experts say that even Thomas Jefferson once toyed with the idea of having a little Gothic "folly" for the family graveyard, but the style did not really become popular until the middle of the nineteenth century. Have any of you ever visited *Lyndhurst* in Tarrytown, New York? If you have, you will recognize some of the same features of that 1838 house designed by the famous Alexander Jackson Davis, only on a smaller scale and in a simpler style, in Dr. Southard's house.

The pointed arches, the gingerbread bargeboards along the edge of the steep gable roofs, the dominant central gable, and the spacious verandas—all of these features were characteristic of what Andrew Jackson Downing in his book on architecture, *Cottage Residences,* called "Rural Gothic Style." You will see a copy of Downing's book in Dr. Southard's library. It must have been a best-seller, because it had twelve printings between 1842 and 1888. Perhaps Dr. Southard was influenced by that book in building his house.

Some people of the time called this style "the architecture of Christianity, the sublime, the glorious Gothic." They associated it with honesty, morality, and religion. Buildings constructed in this style cannot not be called historically accurate, but they did serve to recall what was considered a romantic past, with the pointed arches and oriel windows, and sometimes towers and trellises. Now let us visit Dr. Southard's office.

Doctor's Office (5 minutes) [Let group bypass you and enter first. Stand
      near the parlor door.]
Had you lived in Riverton in the 1850s, you would probably have come to this office many times, either to see the doctor or to get him to return home with you to treat someone in your family. Dr. Southard was the only doctor in town for several years.

He did his part in caring for patients in the city, but his family felt that he really liked country practice better. He loved the peace and quiet of country drives, past other people's orchards and apiaries. They were a happy contrast to what often awaited him at home. His future grandson-in-law, Orlo Ranney, recalled that, as a young boy, he saw Dr. Southard's office filled with men, women, children, and emotions, and nearly always two or three anxious young mothers with sick babies, waiting for the doctor.

The doctor's wife, Hulda, knew what to do to make waiting patients comfortable, but she had to entertain them and feed them, as well. As she grew older, she had less patience with people who were always complaining about their aches and pains. She would say, "Mrs. Jones, when you get to our age, you're bound to wear out."

Today, it is hard for us to realize what doctors of that time had to endure. With no hospitals, no telephones, few experienced nurses, no paved highways, no pace-makers, intensive care units, rescue squads, or x-ray laboratories, the doctor alone carried the awesome responsibility for human life. Doctors were called upon to make many night calls.

Dr. Southard helped found the state medical society in 1870 and became its first president. He was eager for doctors to get together periodically, share their experiences with patients, and listen to papers on some of the latest discoveries, particularly those being made by German scientists at that time. He was much impressed with the work of Justus von Liebig, who did more to introduce laboratory teaching into medicine than anyone else. He particularly found von Liebig's teaching that plants derive their carbon and nitrogen from the carbon dioxide and ammonia in the atmosphere interesting, and that these compounds are returned to the atmosphere by the plants in the process of putrefaction, thus producing a sort of circulation in nature. This was a natural for Dr. Southard, with his devotion to plants. You may recall that, until fairly recently, hospitals used to take flowers out of patients' rooms at night, because they were thought to take oxygen out of the air. They know better, now, of course. The first paper Dr. Southard ever gave before the medical society was on von Liebig.

Dr. Southard was one of the first to have the courage to try out the new discoveries of ether, which occurred in 1846, and of chloroform, in 1847, the first synthetic organic compounds to be used in medicine. Through his efforts, laboratory experiments were introduced into the state medical school, and young men who worked with him when they were preparing for medical school were encouraged to try experiments on their own.

Dr. Southard loved to tell stories about his early experiences as a doctor. "I'll wager I have an experience that few other doctors ever had," he liked to say. "Did you ever have a man come to you and pay your fee for services at his own birth? Well, a young man came to my office and asked if I had been paid my fee at his birth. I remembered that I had not. 'All right,' he said; how much is it, with interest to date?' I told him, and he counted out the cash." Then he would add, "I think Charles B. Hays is the finest young man in this town."

If the parents of the young man *had* paid Dr. Southard for their child's birth, it might well have been with a haunch of venison, a gaggle of geese, or some freshly churned butter—a practice they called "paying in kind," in those days. Hulda always hoped that people would not bring eggs, because she had plenty of laying hens, so many that she put a lot of the eggs down in a brine of salt and water to preserve them for use in the winter. Sometimes she put them in beet juice, which produced a pretty color to use in salads.

This leather case with the pill bottles in it used to be carried by Dr. Southard as he made rounds by horse and buggy. He always carried a roll of sulphur, like this, with him. If he found someone suffering from a sore throat, he would pulverize some of the sulphur, roll a piece of paper into a funnel, and blow it into the person's throat. Believe it or not, sometimes it worked.

Some of you may recall, as a child, having medicine given to you in powder form, wrapped in bits of paper, such as this. And until well into this century, many doctors still rolled their own pills—without sugar-coating, needless to say. You may notice that some of the surgical instruments that are used today are not unlike those used by Dr. Southard.

Are there any questions? If not, do look into the library before we leave.

The Library (2 minutes)
Most of the books in the library are Dr. Southard's medical books, plus some that belonged to Dr. Ranney. In addition, Dr. Southard had a fine collection of books on plants, trees, and bee-keeping. He was obviously interested in the literature contemporary to his time, both English and American. He owned volumes by Tennyson and Browning, Washington Irving, and Walt Whitman, among others.

One of Dr. Southard's daughters was much interested in what was called "elocution," in those days. There are a number of books on how to speak well, including *The Model Orator,* compiled by Henry Davenport Northrup in 1896. The pictures showing how to express various emotions are amusing: there were specific postures one should assume to portray horror, rejection, anguish, and all the other emotions.

You would be interested in McGuffey's *Sixth Eclectic Reader* that Dr. Southard's young daughters used in the one-room school about a mile from here. The introduction covers articulation, inflection, accent and emphasis, instructions for reading verse, the voice, and gesture, followed by selections from everything from Shakespeare and the Bible to the more current Horace Greeley and Ralph Waldo Emerson.

Augusta used to remember that sometimes school was closed for the day because the boys assigned to build the fire in the stove each winter morning would mischievously add a chunk of rubber to the wood.

Nowadays, in education, there is a swing back to individualized instruction. The Southard children got plenty of that in the one-room school they attended. The teacher personally heard each one read and checked each child's mathematical skill, assigning him lessons according to his ability and progress.

Dr. Southard was so concerned because the local school went only through the sixth grade that he enticed a young college graduate from New York State to come out as a tutor for his children. Other parents joined in, and, as a result, helped start a high school for Riverton. To everyone's surprise, the three Southard daughters enrolled in a nearby college for a couple of years. Their brother, Eugene, went on to Rush Medical College in Chicago, but girls were not supposed to require that much education.

When you finish looking, we will move into the parlor.

The Parlor (3-4 minutes) [Lead the group into the parlor from the office. Stand at the west door leading to the hall. Keep the group inside the ropes on the runner.]

Had you been a very special guest of the Southards—the preacher, for example—you would have been entertained in this room, the parlor. Most of the time, it was shut off and not used regularly by the family except for Sunday-night prayers and for weddings and funerals. Oh, when Augusta, Ida, and Mary were old enough to have gentlemen callers, they were received very formally in this room. Augusta used to tell her grandchildren about how distressed her mother was when a rather heavy-set guest would start to sit on that delicate late-Victorian chair in the corner. Hulda would snatch it from under him, much to his consternation.

On that rosewood table with the marble top is the family Bible. The names of all the family members back to the first Huguenots who came to this country in the 1660s are recorded in the center portion between the Old and the New Testaments. To the family's surprise, there is a list of the "black members of the family," giving first names only. They hadn't realized that people in New Jersey held slaves. The Bible also contains an account of the Battle of Monmouth, fought on an ancestor's farm in New Jersey. It is amusing to read that the cook hid her cooking utensils in the manure pile when she heard that the Redcoats were approaching.

This same old Bible was used in family prayers each Sunday night, each child being required to read a few verses and to memorize at least one verse each Sunday.

The Southards had been Presbyterians, as far back as those French Huguenot ancestors. The entire family attended church together every Sunday, and Hulda and the girls usually went to Wednesday-night prayer meetings, as well. William accepted the basic predestination concept of his church, that God plans, directs, and controls all things and that His plans will be carried out; but he rather shocked the Reverend John Dunning, who preached a blistering sermon against the whole concept of evolution after the news of the publication of Charles Darwin's *Origin of Species* in 1859 reached Riverton. The preacher came to call and vigorously hit the table with his fist as he continued his comments. Dr. Southard, with his real interest in science and in experimentation, quietly remarked, "There's no conflict with our beliefs. Evolution is just God's way of carrying out His plans."

The doctors was tolerant of the local Baptists, but thought that they should baptize their infants, rather than waiting until they were old enough to choose for themselves. He did not mind their using his river-front for their immersions. It always sounded like a lot of fun when they held their noses and went in all over.

Augusta, Ida, and Mary were all married in this room, with family friends and relatives crowded in. We shall see Augusta's wedding dress in one of the rooms upstairs. Augusta used to admit, a bit sheepishly, that she was practically "promised" to a young medical student who was working with her father during the summers, but her second cousin, John C. Bloom, from back east, arrived, in his West Point uniform. She simply couldn't resist that uniform, and she married John, instead of the medical student. Their grandson, Ambassador John C. Bloom, deeded this house to the Southard Memorial Foundation.

The weddings here were always happy occasions, but the funerals were quite the opposite. Augusta's daughter Rosa, as a very young child, felt shut out from the older members of the family when her Uncle Eugene died unexpectedly. Children were not supposed to go into the room and look at the body of a dead person lying in a casket. Older people went in and stayed a long time, chatting away rather nervously. They always brought good food that lasted the family for weeks. Rosa solved her isolation, when someone forgot to close the door to the parlor, by climbing part of the way up the stairs and leaning over the railing, so that she could see Uncle Eugene.

The sorrow of losing his only son saddened Dr. Southard. At medical meetings, he was always sympathetic to the younger doctors. They, in turn, were pleased when something they said amused Dr. Southard, and he threw his head back with a hearty laugh. They admired his "reserve of much learning" and his philosophy.

On February 21, 1904, Dr. Southard himself lay in this room, dead at 82, after only two days of illness. One of these young doctors wrote, "I saw Dr. Southard in his casket—it was the face of a saint."

The rosewood table on which the Bible lies, as well as the settee and matching chairs, were in the latest fashion. They were made by the well-known John A. Belter in his New York workshop around 1850 and were a wedding present to William and Hulda. Rosewood was the favorite wood of well-to-do families. The same styles were recreated in mahogany for the less affluent. The pronounced curves, the elaborate, openwork crestrails and siderails, with their naturalistic heavy carving of fruits, flowers, and scrolls, as I am sure you know, are characteristic of the mid-Victorian period—too elaborate for some modern tastes, but they reflect the romanticism of the period. This was a time when people had an earnest, retrospective love of the past, especially of medieval times—anything old, distant, anything that aroused their sentiments and had human interest. They loved landscape pictures, such as the Turner painting above the settee.

Notice how richly tufted and buttoned the upholstery is, and the frequent use of silk plush and horsehair. If you have ever sat on a horsehair settee, I am sure you will agree with young Rosa, that it is "very prickly." The neo-Gothic side chair reflects the same popular style as the house itself. This type of carpet, with huge roses in the pattern, was very popular in those times, also.

Rosa used to be fascinated with that John Rogers group. *Checkers up at the Farm*, which was popular in the 1870s. It is made of plaster. Papier mâché was popular, too. Papier mâché, of course, is a pulp made from paper especially prepared for that purpose, mixed with glue, chalk, and occasionally sand. Then it is pressed, molded, and baked, and finally polished to a very high gloss, making it look like japanned work. The Southards had no tables of papier mâché, but you will notice a number of small figures, such as that monk's head, on the whatnot, along with colorful glass paperweights, ceramic animals, flowers and birds, and other knickknacks popular at the time. In Victorian times, a parlor would not have been a parlor without a whatnot. Stuffed birds or artificial flowers under a glass dome like this were very popular.

Children were taught early to crochet the antimacassars such as you see here on the backs of chairs. They learned to make samplers and other needlework pictures, as well. They also were required to learn to play this huge "square" piano. (It was made in 1851 by Mumms, Lark, and Clark.) It takes a large room to hold a piano that size. Small wonder that they went out of fashion.

When you have finished looking, we will move across the hall to the less formal sitting room.

The Sitting Room (2-3 minutes) [Let the group go into the roped-off portion of the room. Stand in the hall near the door.]

I suppose we might call this a "family room," today. During Dr. Southard's time, the entire family gathered in this sitting room, including not only the immediate family, but a widowed grandmother and a maiden aunt. This was the warmest room in the house, except for the kitchen, because this was heated by an eight-plate stove, such as the one you see standing on sheets of zinc to protect the floor from hot ashes. Hulda and the other women darned socks or braided rugs. The children did their homework or played card games. William more than likely read his favorite newspaper, eager to keep up with the political news. He had been at Jackson, Michigan, on July 6, 1854, when the Republican party held its first convention, where all who were opposed to the extension of slavery were welcomed. Other issues of the time won his support—the possible extension of a railroad to the Pacific, for example. He heartily supported the program on which Lincoln was elected in 1860 and electioneered as he made rounds, visiting his patients. He loved a good argument on the political issues of the day.

The sitting room, as you can see, was a much less formal room than the parlor. That Boston rocker, for example, looks much more comfortable than the elaborately carved chairs in the parlor. The beech bentwood rocking chair came into fashion in the 1860s, after its introduction from Austria. And I am sure you have all heard of the Morris chair. Some of you may have sat in one at your grandparents' house. Remember how comfortable they are, especially with the back lowered against that sturdy rod? They are certainly the forerunner of the modern lounging chair.

You will probably remember from your literature courses that William Morris was a part of the pre-Raphaelite movement in England, along with John Ruskin and others. They were protesting against the mechanical approach to design in the late Victorian period, 1875-1901. They deplored the many curves and the elaborate carving on furniture like the Belter pieces in the parlor. They wanted to return to a more sincere, simple hand-craftsmanship, with a practicality of design and construction. This Morris chair reflects that change in taste. The portrait is of Dr. Southard, painted when he was in his sixties. People always comment on the twinkle in his eye—something contemporaries appreciated.

Let's move back down the hall to the downstairs bedroom. As you go, notice the hallrack, typical of this period, with its hooks for coats, its metal-lined umbrella stand, and its small looking glass. The banjo clock was made by Simon Willard in 1802 and was brought to Riverton by Dr. Southard's father. For years, the family claimed that the mirror, with its rope, spindle, and pineapple carving, had been in the family "from before the Revolution." A grandson, much interested in old furniture, checked it out at the Art Institute in Chicago and discovered that it probably dates from 1810—a very fine piece of cabinetwork, even though it was not so old as his grandparents used to claim.

Downstairs Bedroom (2-3 minutes) [Lead the group back through the hall to the downstairs bedroom. Let the group into the roped-off portion of the room. Standing in the hall near the door.]

This was William and Hulda's room. All of their four children were born in that ponderous sleigh bed, with its panelled rolled-over headboard and footboard curving upward and rolled outward characteristically, as you can see.

There were no hospitals in Riverton in those days. Even if there had been, women rarely went out of their homes to have their babies. Often, midwives were brought in to help with a birth, instead of doctors. Dr. Southard was concerned about the fact that so many women had more babies than their health would permit and than they could care for properly, especially if they were poor. When he had to witness the death of a young mother leaving her large brood of youngsters behind, or the death of a long-wished-for and beautiful baby, it upset him for days.

Long before Margaret Sanger early in this century put up a vigorous fight for birth control, Dr. Southard gave a paper before the state medical society on the work of the neo-Malthusean League and advocated the legal right of physicians to give birth-control advice to parents and the right of parents to regulate the size of their families.

The family used to retire early—with only the light from oil lamps such as you see on the dresser, you can understand why. They rose early, too, to get the fires started in the kitchen stove for the preparation of a hearty breakfast. The children often used to run downstairs in their nightclothes to dress by the warmth of the stove. The horse had to be fed and wood chopped for all of the stoves. This was Eugene's job, unless he could persuade the hired man to do it for him.

There were few closets in those days. Clothes were hung in ponderous wardrobes, such as that walnut one.

Notice the old wooden chest there, next to the wardrobe. Here, William stored his books and other belongings, when, to earn money for medical school, he drive mules pulling barges along the canal.

Some of us, I am sure, recall visiting the home of grandparents and using a Staffordshire bowl and pitcher, such as those on the marble-topped side table. Hot water was a luxury one did not enjoy often. There was little choice between the matching chamber pot and the dash through the cold to the outhouse which you saw near the barn.

Hulda made the double-wedding-ring quilt on the foot of the bed. Some of her friends came in to help with the quilting. The crazy quilt of silks and velvets on the settee tells the story of the family's best wardrobe over the years.

We will go now to the front of the hall and upstairs to the other bedrooms. If any of you do not care to climb the stairs you may sit on the sturdy American-Empire-style sofa, here in the hall. Many people today think that the numerous heavy, clumsy scrolls used as feet on this piece are not very attractive, but back in the middle of the nineteenth century, this style was apparently greatly admired. Designers included a great variety in their illustrated books.

Do watch your step as we go upstairs.

The Front West Bedroom (1-2 minutes) [Lead the group up the stairs slowly to the front bedroom. Let them stand inside the roped-off portion of the room. Stand near the door in the hall.]

The grandchildren usually slept in this room, on their visits to William and Hulda. You will notice that, in addition to the heavily carved mahogany bed, there is a smaller child's bed in a similar style, and a cradle hung from springs and with a canopy. Older children probably were assigned the responsibility of looking after the younger ones when they were visiting their grandparents.

One of their grandchildren, Rosa, recalled always hoping another child would be there in this room when she was. The long, dark halls, with only the tiny lamp at the top of the stairs, were cold and terrifying. And that hair wreath hanging on the wall opposite the foot of the bed was especially scary. She had been told that it was made from the hair of several of her aunts and uncles. The idea petrified her: she was afraid that, if she went to sleep, someone would slip in and cut off her blonde curls to make another garland similar to that one.

The counterpane was hand-knitted, of linen thread, and the coverlet on the child's bed was hand-dyed and hand-woven by a maiden aunt. The quilt at the foot of the bed, made from material printed in squares to simulate patchwork, was a favorite of the children, because of the animals in the center. It was called "Yankee Puzzle."

The children's toys would appeal even to modern youngsters. The demure lady doll was made around 1840. Her sprigged gown, edged with tatting, and her straw bonnet, tied with ribbons under the chin, are all hand-made. Children learned to sew doll clothes for their own dolls and grew up as fine seamstresses. The two little bureaus, one in American Empire style and the other with the flower-and-fruit carvings, matched grown-up furniture of the period. Toys for the boys of the family were a bit more rare, but you will see small ship models, hard gum-rubber balls, engines, martial peep shows, and tumbling toys that were popular with the young men.

When you have finished looking, we will go down the hall and into the side hall. Peek into the other front bedrooms as we go along. Then we will stop at Eugene's room. In the first room, you will see Augusta's wedding dress, that I was telling you about. She must have had a tiny waist. Notice the delicate stitching, the tiny ruffles on the sleeves, and the width of the skirt. The little hat made of ribbons with something like earmuffs for over the ears probably was the latest fashion in the late 1860s.

Eugene's Room (1-2 minutes) [Let the group stand in the roped-off section. Stand just outside the door.]

This is Eugene's room. You will recall that he was Dr. Southard's only son and that he studied to be a doctor, but died at the age of forty. He had great promise as a doctor.

Eugene's younger sister, Mary, had a combination of fear and fascination about her brother's room. It was pretty dark up here, but her curiosity about what her brother would have next in his room overcame her fears. He was an avid collector, particularly of birds' eggs and stuffed animals and birds. He loved to explore the banks of the river and the canal for specimens of wild life that he would bring home. He would prepare and preserve the skins, stuff them, and mount them. He also knew how very carefully to extract the eggs from their shells, so that the shells could be displayed in a glass-covered case, like that, carefully labeled. He once had a live pet squirrel in a cage in his bedroom.

If there are any questions, I'll be happy to answer them before we retrace our steps and go downstairs to the dining room. Please hold on to the railing, as we go down, and watch your step. The patina on that black walnut railing may be the result of generations of children sliding down it. Remember what fun that was!

Dining Room (2-3 minutes) [Lead the group downstairs, back through the hall and into the dining room. Walk slowly and carefully so that the visitors will, too. Have them stand on the runner between the ropes. Stand on the east side of the room.]

In Victorian times, people enjoyed bountiful meals. Usually, the day began with a hearty breakfast—bacon, sausage, or ham, sometimes beef steak, eggs, fried or hash-brown potatoes, griddle cakes with plenty of butter and syrup, or toast, cooked on the wood stove in the kitchen, along with a huge pot of coffee. Eggshells were put into the water with the freshly ground coffee, producing a very clear coffee with a delicious flavor.

The main meal of the day was served at noon. There would be a hearty soup, from that soup tureen with its scenes of the burning of the *Henry Clay* in 1852 near Yonkers, New York, with its big soup ladle of Sheffield plate. This would have been followed by a variety of meats, vegetables, and homemade hot rolls, topped off with hot apple pie with cheese. Supper was usually leftovers—cold meat, potato salad, cheese. Ice cream was a special treat, made from real cream and fresh fruit. The children enjoyed packing the ice and rock salt into the hand-cranked freezer and turning the handle. It was a special reward to lick the dasher, with its generous leavings of rich ice cream.

For everyday, the family ate from these white dishes with small blue flowers around the edge, known as "poor man's Chelsea," or "Grandmother's china." The best china was the set of Crown Darby from around 1810 that you see on the elaborately carved walnut sideboard created by Daniel Pabst in Philadelphia in 1868.

This large, sturdy table could accommodate the family very well and could be expanded by the addition of leaves in the center when company came. And there was plenty of that. Hulda recalled having several preachers as house guests for three days, while they were attending the Presbytery in the area. They seemed to enjoy her cooking. All of them had steadfastly refused even a sip of wine with their meals, so Hulda was amused when they kept asking for more of the brandied cherries she served with hot rolls for breakfast one morning. Of course, she did not tell them about the brandy.

The Southards themselves were not given to drinking "hard liquor," but they always kept several jugs of homemade elderberry wine handy, for "medicinal purposes."

The bellflower celery and spoon holders on the sideboard were of a popular molded design and the coin-silver spoons in the spoon holder have "N. Matson pure coin" stamped on the back. This one with "Rosa" on the handle was given to Rosa on her sixteenth birthday. It was made by A. C. Wortley.

The Springfield rifle over the mantel was the one carried by Captain

John C. Bloom during the Civil War. Because he had attended West Point for two years, he was made a captain at the age of twenty. The old sword was his, also. Rosa recalled that her brothers argued over who would get the sword and who the rifle. When she protested that she wanted one or the other, her brothers said, "Oh, you're a girl. You can't have these. You take the old family Bible." Later, she was glad that she was given that.

As we follow around to the opposite end of the room on the way to the kitchen and pantry, we will get another view of the library. From this door, you can see the portrait of Susan Caryl Southard holding William when he was a small child. Susan's mother had painted their portrait around 1825. From the way William was dressed, one might think he is a girl. Little boys wore dresses similar to that, as late as the end of the nineteenth century.

Kitchen and Pantry (2-3 minutes) [Lead the group into the kitchen; let them look into the pantry. After the interpretation, let them sit either around the kitchen table or on the patio under the grape arbor while they are served hot ginger cookies and homemade cider.]

I am sure that many of you recall the good smells of food cooking on a wood stove like this. It was a lot of work to split the wood, carry it in a woodbasket like this, and tend the fire to keep it from going out. But a wood stove had its advantages. You could keep a pot of navy beans simmering for hours on top of the stove, and then turn them into a bean pot with salt pork, molasses, and a bit of salt, mustard, and sugar, and even an onion, if you preferred, and let them cook all day in the slow oven. That was a Saturday-night specialty for supper. Soups were especially good simmered in a cast-iron Dutch oven, such as this, until the beef shanks fell to pieces and the vegetables had absorbed the flavor.

Meats were brought in from the farm just outside town that William's father had started, back in the 1840s. A tenant farmer ran it. Milk came from there, too, most of the time, though occasionally the Southards had their own cow. The milk was allowed to sit in flat milk pans, like those in the pantry, while the cream—for making butter—rose to the top. Hulda and the other women of the household took turns churning the butter in that wooden churn. William was particularly fond of the resulting buttermilk.

Fruits and vegetables were plentiful from the orchard and the kitchen garden. You will recall seeing the root cellar when we started the tour. Not only the vegetables that could be used in the winter—

carrots, potatoes, rutabagas, and parsnips—were kept there, but barrels of apples and pears were included. It was a daily task in winter to go to the root cellar for the day's fruits and vegetables. William's daughter Ida used to say that she would as soon eat varnish as parsnips, and yet they were always a part of Christmas dinner.

Some of the apples were made into cider with that press in the pantry and stored in glass bottles. One could get a bit tipsy when the cider got hard. Some apples were made into applesauce and canned in glass jars. And peaches, pears, and cherries were boiled in sugar, placed in scalded glass jars, and then cooked in wash boilers such as that on the stove. Ordinarily, clothes were boiled in those and pounded by hand with a clothes pounder, but they served very well for soaking a whole ham or canning fruit.

Bread was allowed to rise in a dough trough such as you see in the pantry. And notice the yellow-ware bowls and pie plates, an early form of oven-proof pottery.

Hulda never understood why her granddaughters always tried to pin her down as to how many cups of this and teaspoons of that went into a recipe. She measured by hand—a handful of flour, a pinch of salt, butter the size of an egg.

The week's schedule was pretty well worked out for the women of the household—washing clothes on Monday, ironing on Tuesday, baking on Friday, odds and ends in between. Rosa could recall that, even in freezing weather, her grandmother hung the clothes outdoors. It was fun to see the men's shirts frozen solid, and the tablecloths stiff as a board.

You are welcome to sit down on the patio (at the kitchen table) for some homemade ginger cookies and cider. Afterwards, feel free to wander in the garden or along the canal. I shall be happy to answer any questions you have about Dr. Southard and his family, or anything more you want to know about this house and the way of life it represents.

(At this point, an interpreter may be able to judge whether visitors have reacted as we hoped—understanding that Dr. Southard made significant contributions to his profession and to the community, and that his house was worth saving, restoring, and interpreting to the public. Interpreters should also be able to sense whether visitors have been stimulated by this encounter with the past, whether they have learned something about the simple, yet more difficult, way of life more than a century ago.)

Suggested Reading

Although the literature on historic site interpretation is still not plentiful, there have been significant additions through the last eight years to supplement the best in previous publications. Though already in need of updating, the best place to start is *A Bibliography of Historical Organization Practices; Interpretation*, compiled by Rosemary S. Reese and edited by Frederick L. Rath, Jr., and Merrilyn Rogers O'Connell (Nashville: American Association for State and Local History, 1978). It covers many of the topics dealt with in this book. A more recent, very useful volume is *An Annotated Bibliography for the Development and Operation of Historic Sites* (Washington: American Association of Museums, 1982), prepared by the AAM Historic Sites Committee as a by-product of its development of standards for accrediting historic sites.

Freeman J. Tilden's *Interpreting Our Heritage*, first published in 1957 by the University of North Carolina Press, was republished ten years later in a revised paperback edition (Nashville: American Association for State and Local History, 1967, 120 pp., illustrations). It continues to be the only other general treatment of interpretation. A highly personal handling of the philosophy and psychology of interpreting sites in the National Park System, it is an inspirational call for the excellent teacher-interpreter combination, and is somewhat more useful to natural sites than to historical ones. Also useful in interpretation of natural areas is Grant W. Sharpe, et al., *Interpreting the Environment* (New York: John Wiley & Sons, Inc., 1976, 566 pp., illustrations).

Edward P. Alexander's *The Interpretation Program of Colonial Williamsburg* (Williamsburg: Colonial Williamsburg Foundation, 1971, 46 pp., paper), continues to be the foundation study of that site's pioneering work in the field. It has now been supplemented by his excellent *Museums in Motion: An Introduction to the History and Functions of Museums* (Nashville: American Association for State and Local History, 1979, 308 pp., illustrations), and his splendid study *Museum Masters: Their Museums and Their Influence* (Nashville: American Association for State and Local History, 1983, 428 pp., illustrations), with informative chapters on Ann Pamela Cunningham, the savior of Mount Vernon, and Artur Hazelius, founder of the first Open Air Museum.

The history of the historic preservation movement has been advanced by the two-volume publication of Charles B. Hosmer, Jr., *Preservation Comes of Age: From Williamsburg to the National Trust, 1926-1949,* (Charlottesville: University of Virginia Press, 1981, 1291 pp., illustrations), a fitting sequel to his earlier *Presence of the Past, A History of the Preservation Movement in the United States before Williamsburg* (New York: G. P. Putnam's Sons, 1965, 386 pp., illustrations). Both works focus more on architectural preservation than on interpretation.

The interpretation of objects in historic sites has benefited from the increasing study of material culture. Within that growing body of literature, three recent volumes are particularly useful: Ian M. G. Quimby, editor, *Material Culture and the Study of American Life* (New York: W. W. Norton for The Henry Francis du Pont Winterthur Museum, 1978, 250 pp., illustrations); Thomas J. Schlereth, *Artifacts and the American Past* (Nashville: American Association for State and Local History, 1980, 294 pp., illustrations), especially chapters 4 and 5; and Thomas J. Schlereth, editor, *Material Culture Studies in America* (Nashville: American Association for State and Local History, 1982, 419 pp.) Interpreters should also be familiar with two works by William Seale: *The Tasteful Interlude, American Interiors Through the Camera's Eye, 1860-1917,* second edition (Nashville: American Association for State and Local History, 1981, 284 pp., illustrations); and *Recreating the Historic House Interior* (Nashville: American Association for State and Local History, 1979, 270 pp., illustrations).

The field of living history has been greatly enriched by Jay Anderson's *Time Machines: The World of Living History* (Nashville: American Association for State and Local History, 1984, 217 pp., illustrations), which discusses ways in which living history has been used at a number of major sites. Of continued usefulness is Daniel B. and Patricia B. Reibel's *Manual for Guides, Docents, Hostesses, and Volunteers of Old Economy,* revised edition (Ambridge, Pennsylvania: Harmonie Associates, 1974, 73 pp., paper). Patricia F. Black's *The Live-In at Old Economy, An Experiment in a Role-Playing Educational Program in the Museum* (Ambridge: Harmonie Associates, Inc., 1972, 42 pp., illustrations), is also helpful. Peter S. O'Connell's "Adolescents and Museums," a project report to the National Endowment for the Humanities (Sturbridge, Mass.: Old Sturbridge Village, 1979, 38 pp., appendices, typed) offers useful observations on dealing with this special audience. The advantages and disadvantages of role-playing by interpreters are discussed in *Interpreting Healy House*, an audiovisual training kit with a 25-page supplemental publication, produced by the American Association for State and Local history (Nashville, 1974), and a thoughtful analysis by Frank Barnes titled "Viewpoint: Living History, Clio—or Cliopatria," in *History News*, XXIX (September 1974): 202-203. See also G. Ellis Burcaw's article, "Can History Be Too Lively?", in *Museum Journal*, LXXX (June 1980): 5-7.

Arminta Neal's *Help! For the Small Museum* (Boulder, Colorado: Pruett Press, 1969, 200 pp., illustrations), and her newer *Exhibits for the Small Museum* (Nashville: American Association for State and Local History, 1976, 169 pp., illustrations), continue to be useful advice for the small site that wishes to create introductory exhibits on a small budget. Carl E. Guthe's *The Management of Small History Museums*, second edition (Nashville: American Association for State and Local History, 1969, 78 pp., paper) continues to be an excellent introduction to the history museum; and Shirley P. Low's "Historic Site Interpretation: The Human Approach" (Technical Leaflet No. 32) and Mary Claire Bradshaw's "Volunteer Docent Programs: A Pragmatic Approach to Museum Interpretation" (Technical Leaflet 65) are useful introductions to their subjects in the AASLH series of Technical Leaflets.

Robert G. Tillotson's *Museum Security* (Paris: International Council of Museums, 1977, 243 pp., illustrations), contains sound recommendations on a subject of growing importance to historic site managers and interpreters.

The process of evaluation is discussed in an excellent article by N. Geoffrey Hayward and John W. Larkin, "Evaluating Visitor Experiences and Exhibit Effectiveness at Old Sturbridge Village," published in *Museum Studies Journal*, I, No. 2 (Fall 1983): 42-51. See also Robert C. Birney's "An Evaluation of Visitor's Experience at the Governor's Palace, Colonial Williamsburg, Virginia," in *Academic Psychology Bulletin*, IV (March 1982): 135-41.

Finally, when the burdens of interpretation grow heavy and spirits need lifting, we recommend quiet time—inevitably interrupted by chuckles—with David Macaulay's entertaining exercise in misinterpretation, *Motel of the Mysteries* (Boston: Houghton Mifflin Company, 1979, 96 pp., outrageous illustrations). Interpretation is a serious challenge . . . but it should also be FUN!

Index